EXECUTIVE OFFICE OF THE PRESIDENT
NATIONAL SCIENCE AND TECHNOLOGY COUNCIL
WASHINGTON, D.C. 20502

February 5, 2016

Members of Congress:

I am pleased to transmit with this letter the National Science and Technology Council's (NSTC) *Federal Cybersecurity Research and Development Strategic Plan*. This plan responds to Section 201 of the Cybersecurity Enhancement Act of 2014, which directs the NSTC and the Networking and Information Technology Research and Development (NITRD) Program to develop a strategic plan to guide Federal cybersecurity research and development. It builds on *Trustworthy Cyberspace: Strategic Plan for the Federal Cybersecurity Research and Development Program*, which was released by the NSTC in December 2011.

As a foundation that enables safety and innovation in cyberspace, cybersecurity is of fundamental importance to the economic strength and national security of the United States. While the United States is increasingly dependent upon cyberspace, cybersecurity has not kept pace with the increase in cyber threats. Advances in cybersecurity science and engineering are urgently needed to preserve the Internet's societal and economic benefits and establish a position of assurance, strength, and trust for cyber systems and professionals. The NSTC's work provides a solid basis for Federal cybersecurity research and development policy. The advances in science and engineering established by this plan will enable fundamental changes in the nature of cyberspace by reversing asymmetric advantages currently enjoyed by adversaries of the United States. The subsequent increase in cybersecurity will enable further innovation, enhancing national security and economic competitiveness. I look forward to working with the Congress and other key partners to realize that goal.

Sincerely,

John P. Holdren
Assistant to the President for Science and Technology
Director, Office of Science and Technology Policy

About the National Science and Technology Council

The National Science and Technology Council (NSTC) is the principal means by which the Executive Branch coordinates science and technology policy across the diverse entities that make up the Federal research and development (R&D) enterprise. One of the NSTC's primary objectives is establishing clear national goals for Federal science and technology investments. The NSTC prepares R&D packages aimed at accomplishing multiple national goals. The NSTC's work is organized under five committees: Environment, Natural Resources, and Sustainability; Homeland and National Security; Science, Technology, Engineering, and Mathematics (STEM) Education; Science; and Technology. Each of these committees oversees subcommittees and working groups that are focused on different aspects of science and technology. More information is available at www.whitehouse.gov/ostp/nstc.

About the Office of Science and Technology Policy

The Office of Science and Technology Policy (OSTP) was established by the National Science and Technology Policy, Organization, and Priorities Act of 1976. OSTP's responsibilities include advising the President in policy formulation and budget development on questions in which science and technology are important elements; articulating the President's science and technology policy and programs; and fostering strong partnerships among Federal, state, and local governments, and the scientific communities in industry and academia. The Director of OSTP also serves as Assistant to the President for Science and Technology and manages the NSTC. More information is available at www.whitehouse.gov/ostp.

About the Subcommittee on Networking and Information Technology Research and Development

The Subcommittee on Networking and Information Technology Research and Development (NITRD), also known as the NITRD Program, is a body under the Committee on Technology (CoT) of the NSTC. The NITRD Subcommittee coordinates multiagency research and development programs to help assure continued U.S. leadership in networking and information technology, satisfy the needs of the Federal Government for advanced networking and information technology, and accelerate development and deployment of advanced networking and information technology. It also implements relevant provisions of the High-Performance Computing Act of 1991 (P.L. 102-194), as amended by the Next Generation Internet Research Act of 1998 (P.L. 105-305), and the America Creating Opportunities to Meaningfully Promote Excellence in Technology, Education and Science (COMPETES) Act of 2007 (P.L. 110-69). For more information, see www.nitrd.gov.

National Science and Technology Council

Chair
John P. Holdren
Assistant to the President for Science and
Technology and Director, Office of Science and
Technology Policy

Staff
Afua Bruce
Executive Director
Office of Science and Technology Policy

Subcommittee on
Networking and Information Technology Research and Development

Co-Chair
James Kurose
Assistant Director, Computer and Information
Science and Engineering Directorate
National Science Foundation

Co-Chair
Keith Marzullo
Director, National Coordination Office for
Networking and Information Technology
Research and Development

Cybersecurity Research and Development Strategic Plan Working Group

Gregory Shannon (Chair)
Office of Science and Technology Policy

Douglas Maughan
Department of Homeland Security

Kathleen Bogner
Office of the Director of National Intelligence

Jayne Morrow
Office of Science and Technology Policy

Jeremy Epstein
National Science Foundation

William Newhouse
National Institute of Standards and Technology

Timothy Fraser
Defense Advanced Research Projects Agency

William Timothy Polk
Office of Science and Technology Policy

Steven King
Department of Defense

Staff
Tomas Vagoun
National Coordination Office for Networking and
Information Technology Research and
Development

William Bradley Martin
National Security Agency

Table of Contents

Executive Summary

Computers and computer networking provide major benefits to modern society, yet the growing costs of malicious cyber activities and cybersecurity itself diminish these benefits. Advances in cybersecurity are urgently needed to preserve the Internet's growing social and economic benefits by thwarting adversaries and strengthening public trust of cyber systems.

On December 18, 2014 the President signed into law the *Cybersecurity Enhancement Act of 2014*. This law requires the National Science and Technology Council (NSTC) and the Networking and Information Technology Research and Development (NITRD) Program to develop and maintain a cybersecurity research and development (R&D) strategic plan (the Plan) using an assessment of risk to guide the overall direction of Federally-funded cybersecurity R&D. This plan satisfies that requirement and establishes the direction for the Federal R&D enterprise in cybersecurity science and technology (S&T) to preserve and expand the Internet's wide-ranging benefits.[1]

This strategic plan updates and expands the December 2011 plan, *Trustworthy Cyberspace: Strategic Plan for the Federal Cybersecurity Research and Development Program*. The 2011 plan defined a set of interrelated breakthrough objectives for Federal agencies that conduct or sponsor R&D in cybersecurity. This Plan incorporates and expands the priorities in the 2011 plan and adds a strong focus on evidence-validated R&D. Evidence of cybersecurity efficacy and efficiency, such as formal proofs and empirical measurements, drives progress in cybersecurity R&D and improves cybersecurity practice.

Four assumptions are the foundation of this plan:

> **Adversaries**. Adversaries will perform malicious cyber activities as long as they perceive that the potential results outweigh the likely effort and possible consequences for themselves.

> **Defenders**. Defenders must thwart malicious cyber activities on increasingly valuable and critical systems with limited resources and despite evolving technologies and threat scenarios.

> **Users**. Users—legitimate individuals and enterprises[2]—will circumvent cybersecurity practices that they perceive as irrelevant, ineffective, inefficient, or overly burdensome.

> **Technology**. As technology cross-connects the physical and cyber worlds, the risks as well as the benefits of the two worlds are interconnected.

The plan defines three research and development goals to provide the science, engineering, mathematics, and technology necessary to improve cybersecurity in light of these assumptions. The science and engineering advances needed are socio-technical in nature, and vary from foundational to applied over a range of time scales:[3]

> **Near-Term Goal (1-3 years).** Achieve S&T advances to counter adversaries' asymmetrical advantages with effective and efficient risk management.

---

[1] "S&T" refers to a broad set of disciplines in Science, Technology, Engineering, and Mathematics (STEM).

[2] Non-malicious.

[3] "Socio-technical" refers to the human and social factors in the creation and use of technology. For cybersecurity, a socio-technical approach considers human, social, organizational, economic and technical factors, and the complex interaction among them in the creation, maintenance, and operation of secure systems and infrastructure.

Mid-Term Goal (3-7 Years). Achieve S&T advances to reverse adversaries' asymmetrical advantages, through sustainably secure systems development and operation.

Long-Term Goal (7-15 years). Achieve S&T advances for effective and efficient deterrence of malicious cyber activities via denial of results and likely attribution.

While near-term goals are frequently focused on developing and refining existing science, medium- and long-term goals require both refinement and improvement of existing science, and fundamental research, which has the potential for identifying transformative new approaches to solve problems beyond the current research areas.

To achieve these goals, the Plan focuses on developing S&T to support four defensive elements:

Deter. The ability to efficiently discourage malicious cyber activities by measuring and increasing costs to adversaries carrying out such activities, diminishing the spoils, and increasing risks and uncertainty for potential adversaries.

Protect. The ability of components, systems, users, and critical infrastructure to efficiently resist malicious cyber activities and to ensure confidentiality, integrity, availability, and accountability.

Detect. The ability to efficiently detect, and even anticipate, adversary decisions and activities, given that perfect security is not possible and systems should be assumed to be vulnerable to malicious cyber activities.

Adapt. The ability of defenders, defenses, and infrastructure to dynamically adapt to malicious cyber activities, by efficiently reacting to disruption, recovering from damage, maintaining operations while completing restoration, and adjusting to thwart similar future activity.

After a description of each element and associated research challenges, the Plan identifies research objectives to achieve in each element over the near-, mid-, and long-term. The objectives are not comprehensive but establish a basis to measure progress in implementing the Plan. These elements are applicable throughout cyberspace, although some objectives are most meaningful in particular contexts, such as cloud computing or the Internet of Things (IoT).

The Plan identifies six areas critical to successful cybersecurity R&D: (1) scientific foundations; (2) enhancements in risk management; (3) human aspects; (4) transitioning successful research into pervasive use; (5) workforce development; and (6) enhancing the infrastructure for research.

The Plan closes with five recommendations:

Recommendation 1. Prioritize basic and long-term research in Federal cybersecurity R&D.

Recommendation 2. Lower barriers and strengthen incentives for public and private organizations that would broaden participation in cybersecurity R&D.

Recommendation 3. Assess barriers and identify incentives that could accelerate the transition of evidence-validated effective and efficient cybersecurity research results into adopted technologies, especially for emerging technologies and threats.

Recommendation 4. Expand the diversity of expertise in the cybersecurity research community.

Recommendation 5. Expand diversity in the cybersecurity workplace.

Implementing the Plan and these recommendations will create S&T for cybersecurity that effectively and efficiently defends cyberspace and sustains an Internet that is inherently more secure.

1. Introduction

The modern computing era arrived less than 70 years ago, with the public announcement in 1946 of the Electronic Numerical Integrator And Computer (ENIAC), first used to calculate artillery firing tables. The Internet era was ushered in 23 years later, when the first two ARPANET nodes were established in 1969. In 1993, the Mosaic browser transformed the Internet into an interconnected web of information. Social media's explosion in the following decade made cyberspace an integral component of society's fabric, and accelerated the adoption of smart mobile devices, which provide Internet access from almost every location. Computing and networking underpin critical infrastructure and form the backbone of modern military systems. Today, information technology (IT) is woven into nearly every aspect of modern life, and emerging technologies of the 21st century, such as the IoT and smart cities, promise that cyberspace will continue to offer exceptional benefits to society even as it continues to evolve.[4]

While computing is only 70 years old, cybersecurity is an even younger discipline. Early computing used large systems in data centers that could be protected by guards, guns, and gates. The Internet erased many physical boundaries, but in its early days, it connected only a small cadre of trusted people in academia and government laboratories. Because access was limited to trusted colleagues and resources on the Internet were of relatively limited scope, security was not a significant issue.

In 1988, the Morris Worm brought the Internet to a standstill, and the significance of cybersecurity became clear.[5] While the Internet is far more robust today than it was in 1988, cyber threats have also increased. Today, U.S. intellectual property is being stolen, critical infrastructure is at risk, commercial and government computer systems are hacked, and consumers are worried about their privacy. As currently deployed, the Internet places both public and private sectors at a major disadvantage with cyber criminals and other malicious adversaries. The more society relies on the benefits of IT, the greater the potential disruption, diversion, and destruction that adversaries can create via malicious cyber activities.[6]

The current trajectories for benefit and risk are unsustainable. One recent report suggests the benefits may be overtaken by cybersecurity costs as early as 2030.[7] Just as brakes enable driving safely at higher speeds, cybersecurity is the foundation that enables economic growth and faster innovation in cyberspace. Advances in cybersecurity are urgently needed to preserve the Internet's societal and economic benefits by establishing a position of assurance, strength, and trust for cyber systems and professionals. Just as Federally-funded research and development (R&D) was essential to the development of ENIAC, ARPANET, and the Internet browser, strategic Federal R&D investments can contribute to these advances in cybersecurity and preserve the benefits it helped create.

---

[4] In this document, "information technology" is intended broadly to include networking and communications, and may be thought of as interchangeable with "information and communications technology," or ICT.

[5] The Morris worm of November 2, 1988 was one of the first computer worms distributed via the Internet. It was the first to gain significant mainstream media attention. It also resulted in the first felony conviction in the United States under the 1986 Computer Fraud and Abuse Act. It was written by a graduate student at Cornell University, Robert Tappan Morris.

[6] Malicious cyber activity is defined as activities, other than those authorized by or in accordance with U.S. law, that seek to compromise or impair the confidentiality, integrity, or availability of computers, information or communications systems, networks, physical, or virtual infrastructure controlled by computers or information systems, or information resident thereon.

[7] "Risk Nexus: Overcome by Cyber Risks?" The Atlantic Council, Pardee Center for International Futures, and Zurich Insurance Group, April 2015. http://www.atlanticcouncil.org/cyberrisks/

On December 18, 2014, the President signed into law the *Cybersecurity Enhancement Act of 2014* (Public Law 113-274). In the second of its five titles, the law requires the NSTC and NITRD Program to develop and maintain, based on an assessment of risk, a cybersecurity R&D strategic plan to guide the overall direction of Federally-funded R&D. This document (the Plan) was developed by interagency subject-matter experts from the NITRD Program and the NSTC, under the leadership of the White House Office of Science and Technology Policy (OSTP). The committee consulted with industry and academia through a Request for Information issued through NITRD and engagements with industry at public conferences to ensure that Federally-funded R&D activities do not duplicate private-sector investments.

This Plan calls for a strong focus on evidence-driven S&T for cybersecurity.[8] Evidence of efficacy and efficiency is needed not only to guide cybersecurity R&D progress, but also to change cybersecurity practice for the better.

This Plan updates and expands the December 2011 strategic plan, *Trustworthy Cyberspace: Strategic Plan for the Federal Cybersecurity Research and Development Program*.[9] That plan defined a set of breakthrough objectives for the agencies of the U.S. Government that conduct or sponsor R&D in cybersecurity. This 2015 plan is more comprehensive, and it incorporates and expands the priorities in the 2011 plan. Both plans demonstrate the maturing Federal approach to cybersecurity R&D as the Nation's demand for effective and efficient cybersecurity grows.

Cybersecurity is a shared responsibility. The private sector, government, and academia all have roles to play in cybersecurity R&D. Government funds long-term, high-risk research and mission-specific R&D. Academia and research institutions perform the majority of this high-risk research. The private sector funds near-term research and transitions successful research into commercial products. This document lays out a research agenda for Federally-funded R&D carried out by government agencies and the U.S. R&D enterprise, informed by interactions with business and academia.

The R&D strategy outlined in this document is shaped by current events, recent Executive Orders (EOs), reports from Presidential advisory committees, and other national policies and initiatives. Specific policy priorities include an emphasis on cybersecurity for critical infrastructure; the incorporation of strong privacy protections into national-security initiatives; information sharing between government and the private sector; and protecting consumers from financial fraud.

The President recognized the dangers in U.S. technology dependence and identified cybersecurity for the Nation's critical infrastructure as an urgent priority in 2013, issuing EO 13636, Improving Critical Infrastructure Cybersecurity[10], and Presidential Policy Directive (PPD) 21, Critical Infrastructure Security and Resilience.[11] Cybersecurity is also featured in the National Preparedness Goal[12] and highlighted in PPD 8 National Preparedness, which identified five mission areas for strengthening security and resilience

---

[8] Evidence is meant to inform and drive both research and practice; it can take forms such as subject-matter-expert opinions, qualitative evidence, models of protection from defined threats, empirical evidence, and mathematical proofs.

[9] https://www.whitehouse.gov/sites/default/files/microsites/ostp/fed_cybersecurity_rd_strategic_plan_2011.pdf

[10] http://www.gpo.gov/fdsys/pkg/FR-2013-02-19/pdf/2013-03915.pdf

[11] http://www.gpo.gov/fdsys/pkg/DCPD-201300092/pdf/DCPD-201300092.pdf

[12] https://www.fema.gov/media-library/assets/documents/25959

against the threats and hazards that pose the greatest risk to the Nation.[13] (For additional information on the relationship of this Plan with PPD-8, see Appendix C.)

In 2013, the President's Council of Advisors on Science and Technology (PCAST) issued the report *Immediate Opportunities for Improving Cybersecurity*. One of the key findings in that report reflects the fragile nature of the IT base:

> *Future architectures will need to start with the premise that each part of a system must be designed to operate in a hostile environment. Research is needed to foster systems with dynamic, real-time defenses to complement traditional hardening approaches, such as firewalls and virus scanners.[14] [15]*

In its 2015 Review of the NITRD program, PCAST further indicated the fragile nature of IT when it recommended broad foundational research and more applied mission-appropriate investigations, on:

> *...methods to facilitate end-to-end construction of trustworthy systems, particularly for emerging application domains, and on ways to anticipate and defend against attacks, engaging not only computer science but also other engineering disciplines and behavioral and social science.[16]*

Another theme is cybersecurity's role as an enabler of privacy. Disclosures of classified intelligence activities and exfiltration of personal information from government and corporate systems created a broad national discussion of privacy and confidentiality in the context of national security and cybersecurity. The January 2013 PCAST report on the NITRD Program cited privacy and protected disclosure as a cross-cutting theme, "...one that is important for every agency and mission, as huge amounts of diverse information about individuals become available in online electronic form." [17]

Another of the key findings from the 2013 PCAST cybersecurity report addressed information sharing:

> *To improve the capacity to respond in real time, cyber threat data need to be shared more extensively among private-sector entities and—in appropriate circumstances and with publicly understood interfaces—between private-sector entities and Government.[18]*

The importance of information sharing for critical infrastructure was also highlighted in PPD-21, and the Administration has encouraged legislative initiatives to address information sharing in other sectors.

Authentication is a recurring theme in recent policy initiatives. The 2011 *National Strategy for Trusted Identities in Cyberspace* (NSTIC) highlighted the importance of privacy,[19] security, and ease-of-use of authentication for sensitive online transactions, and Federal Information Processing Standard 201-2

---

[13] http://www.dhs.gov/presidential-policy-directive-8-national-preparedness

[14] https://www.whitehouse.gov/sites/default/files/microsites/ostp/PCAST/pcast_cybersecurity_nov-2013.pdf

[15] This Plan complements the Critical Infrastructure Security and Resilience (CISR) R&D Plan released in November, 2015. The technical advances envisioned by this strategy apply to the cyber-dependent aspects of our critical infrastructure, furthering the priority areas laid out in the CISR R&D Plan. See https://www.dhs.gov/sites/default/files/publications/National%20CISR%20R%26D%20Plan_Nov%202015.pdf.

[16] "PCAST Report to the President and Congress Ensuring Leadership in Federally Funded Research and Development in Information Technology," August 2015. https://www.whitehouse.gov/sites/default/files/microsites/ostp/PCAST/nitrd_report_aug_2015.pdf

[17] https://www.whitehouse.gov/sites/default/files/microsites/ostp/pcast-nitrd2013.pdf

[18] https://www.whitehouse.gov/sites/default/files/microsites/ostp/PCAST/pcast_cybersecurity_nov-2013.pdf

[19] https://www.whitehouse.gov/sites/default/files/rss_viewer/NSTICstrategy_041511.pdf

established common authentication standards for Federal employees.[20] In 2013, EO 13681, Improving the Security of Consumer Financial Transactions, identified strong authentication as a foundational tool for consumer protection.[21] Policy initiatives involving cyber-physical systems, such as the National Security Telecommunications Advisory Committee (NSTAC) November 2014 report *NSTAC Report to the President on the Internet of Things,*[22] have demonstrated an additional need for more secure authentication of network devices.

This strategic plan is inspired by the context of the events and policy statements described above. The strategic R&D portfolio it lays out will increase the breadth and robustness of cybersecurity measures for IT, and will support the policy priorities highlighted above. The framework and priorities set forth in this Plan must continue to evolve as understanding of threats, challenges, and solutions improves and as new policies are implemented.

The remainder of this document presents the core parts of the Plan, organized in five sections. The first section, Strategic Framing, provides a vision statement, the articulation of challenges, the cybersecurity elements this Plan seeks to establish, and a set of critical dependencies. The next section, Defensive Elements, expands upon the R&D challenges for each defensive element in turn, along with its respective near-, mid-, and long-term objectives. The third section, Emerging Technologies and Applications, relates these elements to emerging technology areas, such as IOT, and provides examples of technology-specific research priorities. The fourth section, Critical Dependencies, details challenges and objectives for the six cross-cutting issues. The fifth section, Implementation of the Plan, outlines the roles and responsibilities of Federal agencies, the private sector, universities, and other research organizations. This section of the Plan also identifies coordination mechanisms within government and with the private sector. The Plan closes with recommendations, as requested in the *Cybersecurity Enhancement Act of 2014.*

---

[20] http://nvlpubs.nist.gov/nistpubs/FIPS/NIST.FIPS.201-2.pdf

[21] http://www.gpo.gov/fdsys/pkg/FR-2014-10-23/pdf/2014-25439.pdf

22

   http://www.dhs.gov/sites/default/files/publications/NSTAC%20Report%20to%20the%20President%20on%20the%20Internet%20of%20Things%20Nov%202014%20%28updat%20%20%20.pdf

2. Strategic Framing

This strategic plan for cybersecurity R&D is based on an analysis of the current and future risk environment, and opportunities for cybersecurity R&D to best address those risks. The strategy focuses on thwarting malicious cyber activities by developing S&T to support four defensive elements—Deter, Protect, Detect, and Adapt—using socio-technical approaches. This strategy is driven by evidence-based evaluations and measurements of the efficacy and efficiency of cybersecurity S&T solutions. They are effective if they achieve the desired security result; they are efficient when the measured units-of-benefit is greater than the minimized units-of-cost. These criteria guide the search for ever-improving solutions from evolutionary and game-changing innovations.

This section lays out an analytic framing based on existing and emerging cybersecurity risks, underlying assumptions, and the primary S&T challenges to define the Plan's vision and goals. The framing then defines the defensive elements and areas of critical dependencies essential to reaching the desired outcome of inherently more secure cyber systems.

Risks

This Plan considers the cybersecurity threats that exist today and those that are likely to emerge in the next 10 years. Current information systems and infrastructure are used in increasingly vital tasks, such as controlling critical infrastructure, but are widely known to possess vulnerabilities that are easy to discover and difficult to correct. Remedies are often expensive to implement, especially at scale. New systems and infrastructure are created with the same weak development processes, introducing the next generation of vulnerabilities. Meanwhile, the Internet and cyberspace in general continue to grow in value, complexity, diversity, and scale, and even traditional companies are becoming IT-intensive. The technical vulnerabilities of cyberspace are exacerbated by inherent and easy-to-exploit human weaknesses that result in on-line and off-line social-engineering manipulations, such as phishing. The many security mechanisms and procedures immediately available are often unreliable or require significant resources to implement. Human resources are constrained by a growing gap in cybersecurity workforce size, diversity, capabilities, and agility.

Adversaries include state actors and non-state actors; their skills and capacities cover a wide range, from amateurish hacks using simple tools to highly sophisticated operators with artisanal tradecraft. Their motivations vary widely, as do the levels of resources they have to pursue their objectives. Given the continued preponderance of easy targets, these adversaries seize opportunities for easy gains. They will continue malicious cyber activities to exploit vulnerable systems, and their sophistication will continue to grow.

Given these risks, this Plan makes four key assumptions:

Adversaries. Adversaries will perform malicious cyber activities as long as they perceive that the potential results outweigh the likely effort and possible consequences for themselves.

Defenders. Defenders must thwart malicious cyber activities on increasingly valuable and critical systems with limited resources and despite evolving technologies and threat scenarios.

Users. Users—legitimate individuals and enterprises—will circumvent cybersecurity practices that they perceive as irrelevant, ineffective, inefficient, or overly burdensome.

Technology. As technology cross-connects the physical and cyber worlds, the risks as well as the benefits of the two worlds are interconnected.

<u>Challenges</u>

The fundamental research challenge is to make cybersecurity less onerous while providing more-effective defenses. The Plan seeks to improve existing technologies and practices to foster secure systems, while at the same time discovering and applying innovations that offer greater ease of use, effectiveness, and scalability that require less cost, human capital investment, and effort to deploy and operate. In this way, users will reap the benefits of IT, improve productivity, and accelerate innovation with fewer risks to themselves and their organizations.

Realization of the Plan requires evidence of cybersecurity efficacy and efficiency; the R&D community needs to establish and achieve measurable cybersecurity objectives. Requiring evidence of efficacy and efficiency is not the same as creating quantitative measures of cybersecurity. Evidence-based approaches require significant work to answer questions such as what can be measured, what data can be collected, and even what is the nature of evaluation in the cybersecurity context. An evidence-based approach for cybersecurity is crucial to identify truly game-changing innovations and is the basis for meaningful feedback loops in evolutionary approaches. The critical need for such evidence applies to all R&D for socio-technical solutions in cybersecurity.

Though it is not the focus of this Plan, it is important for cybersecurity researchers to consider and document the privacy impacts of new cybersecurity technologies and mechanisms to ensure that privacy risks are identified and mitigated at the beginning of and throughout the life cycle of any new cyber mechanism. Privacy cannot exist without the foundation of cybersecurity's confidentiality, access control, and authentication mechanisms, but carelessly implemented cybersecurity controls can negatively impact privacy. A privacy and confidentiality R&D strategy is being developed for release in 2016.

Similarly, policies designed to enforce cybersecurity may be at odds with operating safety-critical systems that must provide continuous operation, such as air-traffic control, flight-control systems, refineries, power grids, and medical devices. In many situations, integrity and availability are the dominant properties of interest. In a degraded system (due to, say, random faults), one may choose to prioritize availability over other considerations. A security-focused policy might prioritize confidentiality or integrity above availability. A systems development framework must be equipped to handle the possible tradeoffs between security and safety considerations. As cyber-physical systems with distributed control authority become prevalent, the difficulty of managing these tradeoffs will increase. This underscores the need for a sophisticated Federal IT cadre of cybersecurity personnel that can continuously evaluate and adapt to the evolving cyber threat landscape, based on evidence, as well as intelligence on the tactics, techniques, and procedures of adversaries.

<u>Vision</u>

If this Plan is successful, the cybersecurity research, development, and operations community will quickly design, develop, deploy, and operate effective new cybersecurity technologies and services, while cybersecurity tasks for users will be few and easy to accomplish. In this environment, many adversaries will be deterred from launching malicious cyber activities, and those that choose to proceed will fail or fail to impact the user or organization's mission.

With the challenge of making cybersecurity less obtrusive and more effective, it is important to remember that when these are lacking, adversaries will have advantages that they will exploit. For cyber adversaries, identifying vulnerabilities and developing ways to exploit them is faster than the lifecycle of developing and deploying fixes for those vulnerabilities, allowing them to stay well ahead of those who protect the systems. This is a classic example of an asymmetric advantage: today it takes far more effort, resources, and time to defend cyber systems than the effort, resources, and time it takes the adversaries to carry out malicious activities. This asymmetry must be reversed.

Integral to this vision for cybersecurity R&D is ensuring that new technologies and applications are put into practice in a timely and efficient way, in order for security measures to keep pace with the emerging tactics, techniques, and procedures employed by adversaries. As part of the Plan's vision to fund research through the full R&D lifecycle—research, development, testing, evaluation, and transition—it aims to identify technologies with a high probability of success that address gaps in critical systems, and to facilitate rapid transfer of research results to potential users, including the dissemination of best practices and outreach activities. Understanding the role of humans as defenders, users, and adversaries is an important (and often underappreciated) aspect of cybersecurity, especially in large IT-intensive enterprises and ecosystems. The Plan envisions partnerships between the research community, the Federal government, industry, and end users, in order to bridge the gap between research and eventual use, and to avoid unnecessarily duplicative public-sector efforts.

Along with an investment in technology solutions, the Plan highlights the importance of investments in the cyber workforce. Achieving the vision will require a diverse workforce of cyber professionals who can design, develop, and implement suitable cybersecurity measures, as well as assessing and managing risk.

Goals

The plan defines three research and development goals to provide the science, engineering, mathematics, and technology necessary to improve cybersecurity in light of these assumptions.[23] The science and engineering advances needed are socio-technical in nature, and can range from foundational to applied, over a range of time scales. The near-term goal provides S&T advances for individual organizations. The mid-term goal applies across organizations, but does not encompass the entire cyber ecosystem. The long-term goal applies to the complete cyber ecosystem.

Near-Term Goal (1-3 years). Achieve S&T advances to counter adversaries' asymmetrical advantages with effective and efficient risk management.

To accomplish this, organizations need a sound understanding of the range of vulnerabilities and threats in cyberspace. This involves evidence-based risk management, which is the process of identifying, assessing, and responding to risk, including the development of effective and measurable controls. Organizations must have access to evidence of the efficacy and efficiency for these controls and consider the human aspects with respect to users, developers, operators, defenders, and adversaries. Achieving this goal will enhance understanding of effective measures against malicious cyber activities and thereby lower their likelihood and overall cybersecurity risks.

Mid-Term Goal (3-7 Years). Achieve S&T advances to reverse adversaries' asymmetrical advantages, through sustainably secure systems development and operation.

This goal is two-pronged: first, the design and implementation of software, firmware, and hardware that are highly resistant to malicious cyber activities (e.g., software defects, which are common, give rise to many vulnerabilities); and second, the development of effective, measurable technical and non-technical security controls that consider human behavior as well as economic drivers associated with cyberspace (e.g., too often system breaches are due to accidental actions by unwitting users). Organizations must improve the efficacy and efficiency of their defenses by several orders of magnitude without placing

---

[23] "Goals" set the overall aims of the Plan and are more generic and all-encompassing in nature than research objectives. "Objectives" in Section 3 are concrete, specific, measurable, and have timelines.

undue burden on users, making malicious cyber activities more difficult, and reducing the rewards of such activities.

Long-Term Goal (7-15 years). Achieve S&T advances for effective and efficient deterrence of malicious cyber activities via denial of results and likely attribution.

Deterrence is the ability to discourage malicious cyber activities by increasing costs, lowering gains, and increasing risks for adversaries. The mid-term goal provides the foundation for increasing adversary effort required for malicious cyber activities and reducing the gains from those activities. Measuring the effort required and the likely results for malicious activities is critical to understanding the degree to which denial effectively deters such activities.

Increasing risks to adversaries requires accurate attribution, which can be difficult, as the origins of individual actions in cyberspace are easy to disguise and verifiable evidence of malicious cyber activity is not always attainable in a timely manner. A high-confidence forensic capacity that identifies the perpetrator within an actionable timeframe, without compromising free speech or anonymity, will increase the likelihood of their discovery and the negative consequences that they will suffer and ideally preemptively cause them to abandon their malicious activities.

<u>Desired Defensive Elements</u>

Given the above goals, the Plan focuses on developing S&T to support four defensive elements:

> **Deter.** The ability to efficiently discourage malicious cyber activities by: measuring and increasing costs to adversaries carrying out such activities; diminishing the spoils; and increasing risks and uncertainty for potential adversaries.

> **Protect.** The ability of components, systems, users, and critical infrastructure to efficiently resist malicious cyber activities, and to ensure confidentiality, integrity, availability, and accountability.

> **Detect.** The ability to efficiently detect, and even anticipate adversary decisions and activities, given that perfect security is not possible and systems should be assumed to be vulnerable to malicious cyber activities.

> **Adapt.** The ability of defenders, defenses, and infrastructure to dynamically adapt to malicious cyber activities by efficiently reacting to disruption, recovering from damage, maintaining operations while completing restoration, and adjusting to thwart similar future activity.

These four elements are similar but not identical to the five core functions in the National Institute of Standards and Technology's (NIST) *Framework for Improving Critical Infrastructure Cybersecurity*.[24] This plan is intended to guide cybersecurity R&D and is therefore broader in scope, while the five NIST core functions are for operational cybersecurity risk management. This Plan discusses risk management as a critical dependency. (Appendix B expands on the relationship between this Plan's four defensive elements and the NIST framework's Core Functions.)

Figure 1 shows how these four defensive elements thwart malicious cyber activities and the value of continuous outcome-driven improvements in efficacy and efficiency.

---

[24] http://www.nist.gov/cyberframework/upload/cybersecurity-framework-021214.pdf

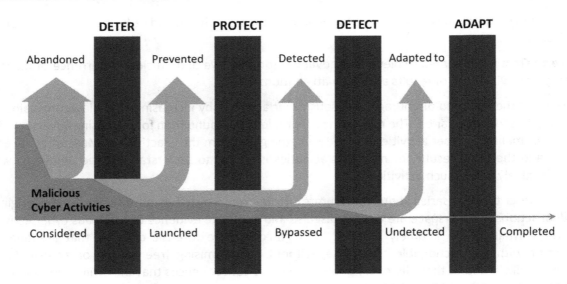

Figure 1. Continuously strengthening defensive elements improves success in thwarting malicious cyber activities.

<u>Critical Dependencies</u>

Advancements in the following six areas are critical to developing the S&T for the four elements:

Scientific foundation. The Federal Government should support research that establishes the theoretical, empirical, computational, and data mining foundation needed to address future threats. A strong, rigorous scientific foundation for cybersecurity identifies methods of measurement, testable models, and formal frameworks, as well as forecasting techniques that express the essential security dynamics of cyber systems and processes. Such foundational understanding is the primary basis for developing effective defensive cyber technologies and practices.

Risk management. Cybersecurity decisions in an organization should be based on a shared assessment of the organization's assets, vulnerabilities, and potential threats, so that security investments can be risk-informed. This must be achieved despite the incomplete knowledge the organization has of its assets, vulnerabilities, exposures, and potential threats. An effective risk management approach requires an ability to assess the likelihood of malicious cyber activity and its possible consequences, and correctly quantify costs resulting from successful exploitation and risk mitigation. Timely, risk-relevant threat intelligence information sharing can improve organizations' abilities to assess and manage risks.

Human aspects. Researchers are capable of developing innovative technical solutions for protecting cyber systems, but those solutions will fail if they do not recognize how users, defenders, adversaries, and institutions interact with technology. Beyond helping to address the challenges of human-system interactions, collaborative engagement of social scientists in cybersecurity research can increase understanding of the social, behavioral, and economic aspects of cybersecurity and how to improve collective risk governance.

Transition to practice. A well-articulated, coordinated process that transitions the fruits of research into practice is essential to ensure high-impact Federal cybersecurity R&D. The research community, which focuses on developing and demonstrating novel and innovative technologies, and the operational community, which needs to integrate solutions into existing industry products and services, are not always aligned. An effective technology transfer program must be an integral part of any R&D strategy and rely on sustained and significant public-private participation.

Cybersecurity workforce. Developing a cybersecurity workforce that can meet the demands described in this Plan remains a key challenge. People are an essential component of cyber systems, and can contribute to security (or insecurity) in a variety of ways. The success or failure of this Plan depends largely upon expanding and retaining a sufficient number of diverse and highly-skilled cybersecurity researchers, product developers, and cybersecurity professionals. In addition, R&D can provide tools to make the cyber workforce more productive—a force multiplier.

Research infrastructure. Sound science in cybersecurity research must have a basis in controlled and well-executed experiments with operational relevance and realism. That requires tools and test environments that provide access to datasets at the right scale and fidelity, ensure integrity of the experimental process, and support a broad range of interactions, analysis, and validation methods. The Federal Government should encourage the sharing of high-fidelity data sets for research and provide protections to those organizations that voluntarily share their sensitive data with researchers. Investments in research infrastructure should support the needs not only of computer scientists and engineers, but also of other sectors with cybersecurity research challenges, such as critical infrastructure in energy, transportation, and healthcare.

Desired Outcome

The value created by computing and networks will continue to be subverted by those seeking illicit gains. IT systems should be assumed to be vulnerable to malicious cyber activities, and perfect security is not possible. Therefore, effective deterrence must raise the cost of malicious cyber activities, lower their gains, and convince adversaries that such activities can be attributed. Having systems succeed in the face of malicious cyber activity is also key, so that they can continue to deliver critical services even when compromised. This strategy will be successful when cybersecurity solutions and technologies provide orders-of-magnitude improvements in effectiveness and efficiency over current approaches. This will eliminate the advantages that adversaries currently have, especially the ability to reuse the same malicious methods across many systems because system defenders are not mitigating vulnerabilities as quickly as the adversary discovers and exploits them. In addition, adversaries leverage current market dynamics where cost and time-to-market are valued more than attention to security. The strategic plan's cybersecurity framing of Deter, Protect, Detect, and Adapt addresses the range of cybersecurity needs, and by doing so, provides a structure for coordinating research and focusing on shared goals. Achieving these outcomes will help lead to a world where the Internet and cyber systems in general are inherently more secure.

3. Defensive Elements

This section describes each of the elements in greater detail, providing a summary of the current state of the art, describing possible impediments, and identifying promising research avenues for each.

Each defensive element also has selected near-term, mid-term, and long-term research objectives. The stated objectives highlight some promising research areas with their expected impact and provide a basis for measuring overall progress in the implementation of this plan. They do not address all areas of need and should not be considered comprehensive. As with the overall goals specified in the preceding section, the target completion of near-term objectives is for 1-3 years from this Plan's publication, mid-term objectives for 3-7 years from publication, and long-term objectives for 7-15 years from publication.

3.1 Deter

The most effective way to secure a system, network, or enterprise from cyber threats is deterrence, the ability to increase the adversary's level of effort required to achieve their objectives and the possible negative consequences of their actions. If adversaries judge that the likely costs of malicious activities, including the risk of prosecution or sanctions, are greater than the expected results, they are more likely to be deterred from attempting the activity. There are a variety of actions that system and network owners, law enforcement, and government agencies can take to enhance deterrence. Deterrence first requires effective and multi-pronged defenses in order to increase the resources required by an adversary. Currently, malicious activities that cause significant impact can be executed for just thousands or tens of thousands of dollars. Proven adversary techniques remain disappointingly effective, and new techniques are quickly packaged into malicious tools requiring only modest technical skill. A successful cyber defense has many facets, ranging from the appropriate technological solutions (e.g., designing secure software, hardware, and operating systems) to network protocols and access controls to human factors, such as instructing users to use safe data handling methods. Cyber defense can be enhanced with more accurate threat models.

Attribution can also dissuade potential offenders. However, identifying the origins of individual malicious actions in cyberspace can be difficult, as the actors are often in a different jurisdiction than the systems they attempt to breach and operate through proxies and other anonymizing procedures. If they successfully breach security, they are often able to delete logs to cover their tracks.

Effective deterrence also relies on the other elements reviewed below—Protect, Detect, and Adapt. Protection means to successfully avoid or ward off malicious cyber activities and prevent damage or disruption of systems, or loss of vital information or even threats to national security. For example, malicious activities are more difficult if software has fewer exploitable vulnerabilities, and hardware and firmware are more tamper resistant. Robust situational awareness, with strong indications and warning abilities, limits the time a successful adversary remains in the system and inhibit lateral movement within the enterprise. Cyber forensics can provide many details about adversaries' methods and identity, exposing adversaries to law enforcement and prosecution. Finally, adapting with resilience means that malicious activities result in minimal disruption of operations and minimal financial or security losses. Adaptive strategies include sharing information about adversaries' techniques and corresponding mitigations quickly with other defenders; temporarily isolating critical systems and networks in encrypted enclaves; or requiring that using (stolen) personal data requires a second authentication step that is difficult to spoof. Protection, detection, and adaptation all contribute to deterrence by increasing the costs and decreasing the results of malicious activities.

<u>Challenges</u>

Malicious cyber activities occur in the virtual domain, but governments impose costs in the "real world." Financial sanctions may be applied to people, companies, and state entities, not to email addresses or computer accounts. While the ability to attribute malicious activity to a specific actor through long-term analysis has improved dramatically in recent years, allowing for such actors to be held responsible for their actions, high-confidence attribution in real-time remains challenging. Another challenge is developing forensic techniques robust enough to preserve evidence suitable for use in legal proceedings, while also bolstering immediate detection and cyber analytical abilities.

The key technical challenge for this aspect of deterrence is quantifying the resources an adversary would require to successfully breach or evade cybersecurity controls or detection. Threat modeling is one way to accomplish this.

To meet these challenges, new technologies are needed to measure and verify the ability of the enterprise to thwart adversary efforts, and to ensure that law enforcement, government agencies, and system and network owners can successfully attribute malicious activities to their source. Examples of these technologies are:

Measurement of adversary level of effort, results, and risks. Measurement provides the feedback essential to improving defenses and to assessing the overall ability to thwart malicious cyber activities. Adversary level of effort could be measured in dollars (if an exploit can be purchased on the black market, contracted out, or fashioned from the salaries of in-house staff), in person-hours of effort, electrical power, or computing resources (e.g., petaflops and terabytes). Where adversaries are deterred because the level of effort is too high relative to the available capacities, the potential gains, or the risks of consequences from malicious activities, they are likely to consider and pursue alternative forms of action. Thus, a corollary to measuring adversary level of effort would be assessing and costing possible alternative actions so as to better anticipate them.

Effective and timely attribution. Accurate attribution of malicious cyber activities to their sources opens up a broad range of response options, such as sanctions, prosecution, and even military actions in appropriately limited circumstances.

Robust investigative tools. Effective investigative tools for law enforcement create the basis for evidence required for successful prosecution of cyber adversaries. These tools must be sufficiently robust to stand up as evidence in court. Alternatively, law enforcement must have valid options to demonstrate the chain of custody without revealing sources or methods.

Information sharing for attribution. Effective mechanisms for sharing information to support efficient attribution are needed to support investigations that cross international or domestic law enforcement jurisdictions.

<u>R&D Objectives</u>

Near-term:

- Establish quantifiable metrics of adversary level of effort needed to overcome specific cybersecurity defenses, as well as assess the viability and cost of alternative courses of action to achieve the same or similar objectives.

- Determine what probability of attribution and criminal or economic sanctions would be necessary to deter various types of malicious cyber activities and adversaries.

Mid-term:

- Automatically extract information about malicious cyber activities to document, verify, and share among law enforcement agencies and other partners to support attribution in near-real time.

Long-term:

- Accurately and efficiently attribute malicious cyber activities to specific actors, companies, or nation states, with sufficient precision to support imposition of costs or economic sanctions and sufficient probability to deter malicious activities.

3.2 Protect

The second defensive element, Protect, focuses on creating systems and networks that are highly resistant to malicious cyber activities through assurance-based engineering practices, which will simultaneously protect a system and supply the verifiable evidence needed to support its assurance case.

Today, virtually every computing system is vulnerable to some form of malicious cyber activity. While continuous improvements in system security are being made, progress is often ad hoc and difficult to measure. Many products have been shipped with large numbers of vulnerabilities,[25] and security controls can be circumvented in practice (e.g., by social engineering).[26] As a result, adversaries find the level of effort required to penetrate systems and networks acceptable in many cases.

Commercial software products that make up a typical computer or mobile device include millions of lines of code, many of which are carried over into successive generations of software through open-source repositories. These products are estimated to include one software defect for every thousand lines of code.[27] Some of these defects create security vulnerabilities, resulting in a cyber ecosystem that is difficult to defend, in spite of efforts to deploy strong security controls and protocols. The security of web servers and many other products are often undermined by small but subtle software coding errors, as illustrated by the "Heartbleed" vulnerability.[28]

Vulnerabilities in hardware design appear to be less common than in software, primarily because of structured design techniques, but they can be more serious, potentially allowing adversaries to bypass protections.

Hardware and firmware may have vulnerabilities such as timing errors, surreptitiously added logic, or information leaks. Achieving effective hardware and firmware protection will require advances similar to those required for software. Today, the exploitation of software vulnerabilities generally precedes malicious cyber activities on hardware or firmware (e.g., adversaries gain system or application level access, then leverage that to penetrate the hardware and maintain a persistent presence). Reductions in

---

[25] As of December 2015, 45 applications and operating systems had more than 250 vulnerabilities listed in the Common Vulnerabilities and Exposures (CVE) database. See https://www.cvedetails.com/top-50-products.php?year=0

[26] For example, the "2015 Verizon Data Breach Investigations Report" states "For two years, more than two-thirds of incidents that comprise the Cyber-Espionage pattern have featured phishing." See http://www.verizonenterprise.com/DBIR/2015/.

[27] For example, in the 2014 Coverity Scan Report, the defect rate is 0.76 per thousand lines of source code for commercial software. See http://go.coverity.com/rs/157-LQW-289/images/2014-Coverity-Scan-Report.pdf

[28] Described at http://heartbleed.com/ and https://en.wikipedia.org/wiki/Heartbleed.

software vulnerability, without corresponding reductions in the number of vulnerabilities in hardware and firmware, will only shift adversaries' focus.[29]

Given a system with a manageable number of security vulnerabilities, achieving high resistance to malicious cyber activities will require effective and efficient security controls and protocols. Cryptographic algorithms, for example, offer quantifiable levels of resistance to specific malicious activities, when implemented correctly. This known level of resistance allows designers to select the appropriate algorithm for a particular system or application.

Many current security controls offer limited or undocumented efficacy, place a burdensome workload on administrators and authorized users, or rely on unrealistic assumptions about the environment or user behavior. All too often, security controls are implemented without proof of effectiveness and imposed on an unwilling user community in an environment that differs radically from the developer's expectations. Current best practices rely on firewalls and virtual private networks to establish a virtual castle, but users' susceptibility to phishing provides adversaries with an alternative entry point.[30] Multi-factor authentication increases security by increasing attack complexity, but users have largely rejected this effective approach to authentication as too cumbersome, particularly when faced with different authentication tokens on different systems.[31]

Challenges

Strengthening protection requires increasing assurance that the products people develop and deploy are highly resistant to malicious cyber activities, because they include very few vulnerabilities and offer effective and efficient security controls to enforce security policies.

Limiting Vulnerabilities

Limiting the number of vulnerabilities in products is a challenge, because vulnerabilities can be introduced at any stage of the product lifecycle. There are five essential aspects needed to produce software, hardware, or firmware with fewer defects that present security vulnerabilities: (1) designing with security in mind; (2) using tools and techniques that produce code with fewer vulnerabilities; (3) testing to identify remaining vulnerabilities; (4) correcting flaws in deployed products; and (5) ensuring that the deployed product is genuine and does not include unwanted functionality.

Design for security. In many cases, security vulnerabilities are present from the start. To avoid systemic security vulnerabilities, system architects must begin with accurate threat models, a well-defined deployment environment, and a robust understanding of the intended application. On this foundation, the architect must apply well-established security principles (e.g., minimizing the privileges required for a system action) and reliable mechanisms (e.g., cryptography, fine-grained access control) to ensure that all components and processes maintain confidentiality, integrity, and availability as appropriate for the application. Ideally, the architect's designs would be implemented without flaws that make them

---

[29] Shifting adversary attention to hardware or firmware exploits will increase costs to the adversary, so reductions in software vulnerability alone would deny some malicious activity.

[30] For example, the 2015 Verizon Data Breach Investigations Report states, "For two years, more than two-thirds of incidents that comprise the Cyber-Espionage pattern have featured phishing." Available from http://www.verizonenterprise.com/DBIR/2015/

[31] To overcome multi-factor authentication, adversaries must perform a combination of on- and off-line exploits to obtain each of the authentication tokens (e.g., password, fingerprint, or physical token), or be in control of the system where authentication data is submitted to piggyback on the authentication event (e.g., to cryptographically sign a challenge). Single-factor systems can often be compromised through the single vector.

vulnerable, but it is not practical to construct systems that are entirely free of security flaws. Architects must assume that the system will include faulty or malicious components and design the system to maintain security properties during the course of computation.

Achieving this vision will require advances in research:

- Architectural assurance tools for precise threat modeling and definition of complex deployment environments, such as Bring Your Own Device (BYOD) policies, cloud computing, and IoT.

- Policy design tools that can derive and verify fine-grained implementation policies for least privilege (e.g., detailed access controls for each file or resource) from human-readable mission policies and objectives. Fine-grained least privilege can substantially reduce what an adversary can accomplish after an exploit.

- Broadly applicable techniques for evidence-based assessment of efficacy and efficiency for the mechanisms currently available to enforce these principles. Where efficacy and efficiency of existing mechanisms is lacking, new techniques for enforcing security principles will be needed. (Some specific examples appear below under the subheading, Enforcing Security Principles.)

- Verified computation techniques that seek to attain secure, authenticated computation using untrusted components. Published results have established the theoretical feasibility of such approaches, but much remains to be done to bring such techniques into practical use.

- Design tools for effective cyber hygiene, in order to improve detection and make it harder for adversaries to hide or persist.

Build secure. Implementation errors can undermine the security of well-designed components. Although common vulnerabilities such as buffer overflows and memory leaks are well understood by most developers, they are difficult to completely eliminate in practice. Existing tools and practices that prevent developers from creating specific security vulnerabilities, or at least make it easier to identify and correct them, are imperfect and inefficient. To reduce the number of common vulnerabilities in products, tools and practices for software and hardware development are needed that have significantly lower impact on developer productivity and operational system performance.

Formal methods for analyzing software during the development phase would enable implementers to identify less obvious vulnerabilities and would also facilitate detecting vulnerabilities in existing software. Formal methods include a broad array of automated reasoning tools, such as constraint solvers and static program analyses. The applicability of these techniques is currently limited to modest programs with tens-of-thousands of lines of code. Improvements in efficacy and efficiency may make it possible to apply formal methods to systems of practical complexity, resulting in new software systems with fewer vulnerabilities.

Verify security. Even when products are designed for security and robustly built, implementation errors will creep in during system development. In addition to functional testing, components should be subjected to rigorous security analysis throughout the development process before deployment. Static analysis tools evaluate source code or executable computer binaries to identify security vulnerabilities. Fuzzing tools present software with unexpected inputs to identify buffer overflows, system crashes, and other exceptions that can lead to denial of service or system vulnerabilities. Because adversaries also use these tools to find zero-day vulnerabilities (software vulnerabilities that are unknown to the vendor), rigorous application of these tools prevent malicious cyber activities by identifying and eliminating vulnerabilities before a product goes to market.

Maintain security. Inevitably, even software that is well-designed, implemented by knowledgeable developers with good tools, and subjected to comprehensive security testing will still have defects. When errors are identified, the software must be updated. The mechanisms used to update software can unintentionally introduce vulnerabilities instead of eliminating them. A secure mechanism for updating software or firmware is an essential aspect for securing products throughout their lifecycle.

Verify authenticity. The four aspects listed above offer the potential to dramatically reduce the number of vulnerabilities in hardware and software, but only if users deploy authentic, unaltered products. Objective measures for supply-chain assurance are needed to increase an organization's ability to confirm that products are genuine, have not been modified, and do not include additional unwanted functionality. Design and manufacture of computing and communications hardware and software are done globally, and the supply chains are made up of diverse interactions among suppliers, integrators, and servicers. The complexity of this supply chain creates opportunities for adversaries to insert counterfeits, tamper with products, and introduce malicious software and hardware. These malicious cyber activities are difficult to detect, and are believed to provide adversaries with more persistent access than malware.

Current best practices for supply-chain management are focused on subjective attributes (e.g., country of origin), despite uncertain efficacy. Research into objective measures for supply-chain assurance (e.g., cryptology-based markers) is needed to better identify genuine products or those that have not been modified and do not include unwanted functionality. In addition, new hardware mechanisms are needed to ensure both hardware and software authenticity. Hardware, firmware, and software offer different challenges for supply-chain assurance, and unlike development assurance, techniques may not apply across multiple sectors.

Enforcing Security Principles

As noted above, under Design for Security, new techniques for enforcing security principles are needed where efficacy and efficiency is lacking in current mechanisms. Several important examples are listed below:

Authenticate users and systems. User authentication is a traditional building block for enforcement of security policy, but deployment of strong multi-factor authentication systems continues to present challenges. Increasing the efficiency of multi-factor authentication to meet user expectations is a key research priority. The proliferation of IoT and autonomous systems increases the need for strong and efficient authentication of devices.

Access controls. Access controls build upon authentication to support the implementation of security policies and authorizations. Systems often rely on coarse grained access control even though more robust mechanisms (e.g., role-based access control) are available. To accurately enforce security policies, improvements in efficiency are needed for system administrators. In particular, new lightweight hardware security mechanisms to enforce integrity and separation would establish a practical foundation for access control.

Cryptographic mechanisms to data. When other protection mechanisms fail and an adversary gains access to IT systems, or when data are transmitted across networks where eavesdropping is possible, cryptographic methods deny access to plaintext and ensure that adversary modifications do not escape notice. Effective cryptographic mechanisms exist for many applications, but they may not work in constrained environments, such as extremely lightweight systems used in IoT. Researchers can also create more effective cryptographic methods in niche applications. While decryption of data is currently required to perform system operations or modifications, thus creating opportunities for a patient adversary, more efficient techniques that operate directly on encrypted data would offer greater security and privacy. The security offered by common cryptographic algorithms could be weakened or defeated entirely by the advent of quantum computing. Although the timeframe for practical deployment of quantum computing remains unclear, protecting highly sensitive information from such systems will require the development of efficient and effective quantum-resistant algorithms.

Mitigate vulnerabilities. Current systems include many legacy components with undiscovered and unmitigated vulnerabilities, and this may be the case for some time. Game-changing technologies are needed to neutralize malicious cyber activities on legacy systems. Data analytics, the science of examining raw data in order to draw conclusions about that data, offers new opportunities to capitalize on security data and identify malicious activities in the absence of established signatures.

R&D Objectives

Near-term:

- Develop secure update mechanisms that support the full range of product formats (i.e., proprietary and open source), applications (e.g., enterprise services and IoT), and lifecycles.

- Develop tools and techniques for evidence-based assessment to determine the efficacy and efficiency of widely-available protection technologies.

- Make cryptographic tools and techniques available for constrained environments (e.g., lightweight cryptography), privacy-preserving applications (e.g., private databases), and long-term confidentiality (e.g., quantum-resistant cryptography).

Mid-Term:

- Create tools for static and dynamic analysis that reduce vulnerabilities in traditionally developed code bases to one defect per ten thousand lines of code (reducing the number of vulnerabilities in new and legacy code bases by a factor of ten).

- Develop automated tools and techniques to derive fine grained security policies implementing least privilege from high-level, mission-oriented policy.

- Develop tools and techniques to verify authenticity and provenance of software and firmware with 98 percent accuracy.

Long-term:

- Create tool chains that support development of software with one defect per hundred thousand lines of code with a relative efficiency metric of 90 percent for productivity and system performance (i.e., systems with 1 percent of the defects in current systems that take no more than 10 percent longer to implement and run up to 10 percent slower than unprotected systems).

- Enhance efficacy and efficiency of security controls, as demonstrated by evidence-based assessment tools and techniques, by two orders of magnitude over 10 years.

- Demonstrate repeatable methodologies for correct computation.

3.3 Detect

Deterrence and protection mechanisms aim to reduce the number of malicious cyber activities attempted and the percentage of those malicious activities that have any significant impact. As long as IT systems store or transmit data of value or manage critical cyber-physical systems of strategic value, malicious cyber activities will continue to be launched, and some number of those activities will warrant detection.

Detection seeks to ensure that system and network owners and users have situational awareness and understanding of ongoing (authorized and malicious) activities, and move towards largely automated detection and warning abilities.

Large-scale cyber situational awareness and understanding remain a challenge today. According to the 2015 Mandiant data breach report, the median time that adversaries were present on a victim network before they were discovered was approximately 6 months.[32] The actual situation is worse, because this does not include breaches that were never detected. Organizations still have difficulty detecting breaches. In 2014, only 31 percent of the organizations that responded to Mandiant had discovered the intrusion themselves; the remainder learned of the intrusion from an external source.

State-of-the-art approaches to cyber defense typically focus on the detection of known cyber events and related artifacts in the later phases of malicious activity; analysis is often ex-post in order to investigate and discover new indicators from the earlier phases. As malicious cyber activities have increased and methods have evolved over the years, established approaches (e.g., signature-based detection, anomaly detection) have not adequately enabled cybersecurity practitioners to stay ahead of these threats.

The gap between aspirations for detection and the current state of detection is striking. It is clear that defenders are not detecting malicious cyber activities at the earliest possible time. It seems very likely that many completed and ongoing malicious activities are never detected; some are probably completed and the tracks are cleaned up, while others likely continue to this day.

Challenges

Enterprise systems and networks are highly complex, with a variety of users in disparate and often dynamic roles. In theory, continuous monitoring of users and timely review of audit logs allow a system owner or operator to discern the presence of current users, how they are connected, and what they are doing. In practice, system owners and operators will require improvements in fidelity and efficiency to make full use of these tools. Adding to the challenge is the volume of information that must be understood in real time. Establishing and maintaining situational awareness and understanding is a challenge, but is an essential first step towards detecting malicious cyber activities.

While researchers envision a future where most detection will be done automatically at machine-to-machine speed, it will still be a challenge to present all components and interactions of a network, IT enterprise, or cyber ecosystem in a way that enables the humans that oversee these systems to have sufficient situational awareness and to intervene as necessary.

Another challenge is differentiating malicious cyber activity from authorized operations. Operations are highly dynamic, and context is significant; for example, actions that are authorized and appropriate during fiscal end-of-year closeout for a start-up might be malicious activity two weeks before an initial public offering. As a result, current tools have many false positives and false negatives. Many techniques for recognition of malicious cyber activities are also retrospective in nature: these tools look for malicious

---

[32] Mandiant Threat Report, "M-Trends 2015: A View from the Front Lines," February 2015, Pg. 3.

activities that conform to a known historical pattern (called a signature). Such tools are rendered useless when faced with innovation by an adversary.

A similar challenge exists with malware detection. Signature-based techniques have value because the vast majority of malicious cyber activities reuse software, but by definition they cannot detect the previously unknown or unaccounted for. In addition, polymorphic malware is specifically designed to circumvent signature-based detection. As with intrusion detection, current tools are not designed to deal with unanticipated methods.

Another difficulty is assessing the limits of the protection element as deployed in a system or network. As with physical security, identifying weaknesses in the cyber environment informs the choice of detection means. For physical security, this may involve better locks or security cameras at weak points. For network security, this might indicate the needed level of detail in system logs or where to install a monitoring system. This assessment is commonly performed by "red teams," but qualified personnel are scarce, and the results vary widely.

To address these challenges, new technologies must be developed that:

Enable robust situational awareness. Systems and networks are highly complex, and device mobility increases complexity. To defend networks and systems, it is necessary to identify all critical assets contained within, when devices have been added or removed, and attributes and anomalies associated with the users. Real-time change detection, including schemes that are flexible enough for dynamic network conditions and that enable comparisons against last known good system states, is essential.

Identify weaknesses in systems. Changes in system configuration, introduction of new applications, or discovery of new techniques may reduce the level of protection or create new vulnerabilities. Tools are required to identify shortcomings in protection measures in near real time, so the situation can be remediated.

Reliably detect malicious cyber activities. Paradoxically, many security tools can detect known malware and previously identified sequences of operations, yet the vast majority of damaging malicious cyber activities still rely on those well-known vectors. Research is needed to determine whether these security tools are ineffective or under-utilized. Regardless of how well they work, these techniques were not designed to detect innovative or unanticipated methods. Additional R&D is required to ensure that the techniques can reliably detect the full range of adversaries' malicious cyber activities and reduce detection time. In particular, tools are needed that can detect zero-day malware and innovative sequences of operations with acceptable levels of false positives and negatives. Behavioral intrusion detection and heuristic tools, which look for anomalies to system baseline activities, offer an avenue of promising research.

Data scientists have recently developed data-mining techniques consisting of scalable mathematical techniques capable of extracting useful information from extremely large data sets. Researchers are learning how to apply these techniques to large volumes of network logs. If successful, this could lead to new, more effective, and quicker detection techniques for malicious cyber activities.[33]

---

[33] When such techniques mature, agencies leveraging them will need to ensure compliance to the Federal Agency Data Mining Reporting Act.

R&D Objectives

Near-term:

- Discover and apply automated tools to map networks, including entities, attributes, roles, and logical relationships between processes and behaviors.

- Develop usable presentation interfaces that allow operators to better anticipate incidents, discover them in progress, and achieve better post-incident response.

Mid-term:

- Use data analytics to identify malicious cyber activities and differentiate them from authorized user behavior with low false positive and false negative rates.

- Apply predictive analysis techniques across a range of potential cyber-threat vectors (e.g., via software or hardware) and determine the probable course of action for each threat method. Predictive analysis supports all four defensive elements: Deter, Protect, Detect, and Adapt.

Long-term:

- Develop automated tools for cyber threat forecasting in order to assess the limitations of protective measures and better inform sensor deployment.

3.4 Adapt

Resilience—the ability of cyber systems and cyber-dependent missions to succeed in the face of malicious cyber activities—is emerging as a critical component of cyber defense strategies.[34] Systems with resiliency continue to perform correctly during and after such activities and recover from adverse effects. To sustain resiliency, systems must also dynamically adapt to changing threats and technologies and withstand malicious cyber activities without substantial damage. This resilience should be embedded in components, systems, and systems of systems (and into supporting lifecycle processes, governance, and operations), so that cyber adversaries are deterred because they perceive that the likely gains from malicious cyber activities are outweighed by the costs.

Preparation for malicious cyber activities can be achieved via protection, supported by detection, and the sharing of threat intelligence information. Effective defense entails the ability to respond, recover, and adjust. Cyber defenders must respond rapidly and effectively to adversary activities, which can range from precisely targeted to global-scale operations. Systems must withstand these events, so that critical mission and operational functions meet minimum performance requirements. When an adversary penetrates a system, response options may include segmentation and isolation (quarantine), fail-over to backup or alternate systems, and hand-off of key functions to entirely different systems or manual processes. Because of the complexity of cyber ecosystems, disrupted functions may require substantial recovery efforts within times determined by the criticality of the functions. Recovery options include autonomic self-repair, restoration from quorum-authenticated backup, and transition to new and secure systems. Adjusting involves cyber defense, systems engineering, and organizational risk management. Ongoing and meaningful threat intelligence and lessons learned from past encounters can help inform

---

[34] The term "resilience" means the ability to prepare for and adjust to changing conditions and withstand and recover rapidly from disruptions. Resilience includes the ability to withstand and recover from deliberate attacks, accidents, or naturally occurring threats or incidents.

cyber defenders' future courses of action. Systems-engineering processes need to apply resilience design principles and make trade-offs among alternative resilience-enhancing technologies to produce more resilient systems and missions. Security should be viewed not as a state of perfection to be achieved and maintained, but rather as a flexible, ongoing process of self-evaluation and informed actions, adjusting to the threat as it evolves.

Mature resilience leverages existing approaches for recovery from natural and other non-malicious incidents, whereas emerging resilience design principles and methods take into consideration adversary-directed actions. These include design principles applied to enterprise information technologies and to internal industrial control systems; forensic analysis methods to extract observables and indicators to guide future courses of action from an existing cyber playbook; automated reconfiguration and recovery mechanisms (oriented toward enterprise IT); deception environments to obtain threat intelligence and misdirect adversaries; and research in trusted foundations, fault tolerance,[35] and adaptive defenses.

Challenges

As cyber security technologies are integrated into complex systems and systems of systems, responses often have unforeseen dependencies and coupled interactions. Developers and users need visibility and insight into these system behaviors, as well as analytic techniques and response pathways that maintain clarity and trust and avoid unintended consequences.

Modern IT systems were often designed according to decades-old principles developed when compute cycles and memory were expensive resources that had to be conserved at the expense of other concerns—including cybersecurity. Today, compute cycles and memory are comparatively cheap, so new design principles are needed that take into consideration ongoing cybersecurity research, the persistence of legacy systems, and the continued adoption of disruptive technologies (e.g., IoT). While comparatively cheap compute cycles and storage establish new opportunities for each of the defensive elements, the opportunities for adaptation and resilience are particularly striking. Ongoing cybersecurity research is exploring new clean-slate design approaches, including new hardware architectures that eliminate broad classes of exploitable vulnerabilities by explicitly maintaining the distinction between executable code and data, and new software that introduces diversity among instances of applications. Some approaches are inspired by biological immune systems, creating cyber systems that continue to function in the face of malicious cyber activities and acquire immunity to new methods by learning from past compromises. Systems designed with these clean-slate approaches will continue to interact with legacy systems and technologies, so new design principles must consider the need to achieve resilience in heterogeneous systems that contain suspect components.

Another challenge comes from the increasing use of autonomous systems, which must also be able to support response, recovery, and adjustment with little or no interaction with (or even knowledge on the part of) cyber defenders. Further, adversaries might co-opt or exploit autonomous functions, and the machine learning that underlies them. The implications of autonomy must be considered as resilience design principles and technologies are created.

Multi-scale risk governance presents technical challenges to current cyber defense activities. Decisions that increase, decrease, or shift factors that contribute to risk are made at many levels and at multiple scales. Decisions made at one level can affect other levels in complex and not always obvious ways. Technical approaches are needed to identify and understand risk dependencies and explore the resulting decision space. Another challenge is that the time within which decisions must be made and implemented

---

[35] Byzantine quorum systems ensure the availability and consistency of replicated data sets in the presence of arbitrary faults.

continues to shrink. In this ever-tightening risk management cycle, information sharing and coordination among decision makers becomes increasingly crucial.

Therefore, to improve the overall ability of systems to adapt, R&D activities should improve the capacity of systems, enterprises, and critical infrastructure to respond, recover, and adjust in three ways:

Dynamic assessment. Measure key properties and attributes of system components and assess potential damage in a trustworthy manner, thereby enabling response and recovery to a known good state. Dynamic assessment means doing this in the context of evolving threat methodologies and system requirements. Focus areas include:

- Real-time digital forensic analysis methods that can provide cyber defenders with insight and understanding of the tactics, techniques, and procedures employed by adversaries. These include methods and tools for the analysis of digital media, data, devices, and network data, and that apply to newer technologies such as mobile, embedded systems, IoT, and distributed cloud services, as well as traditional IT and industrial control systems.

- Real-time assessment of changes, behaviors, and anomalies to enable cyber professionals and other decision makers to make accurate damage assessments, predict and manage potential effects on operations, and determine when system anomalies indicate malicious activity.

- Discovery and analysis of system components and interdependencies (including those injected by adversaries in supply-chain-based malicious cyber activities) to provide insight into how changes in them can affect missions or business functions at multiple scales and timeframes.

Adaptive response. Provide methods to adjust to actual, emerging, and anticipated disruptions, so that mission and organizational needs can continue to be met, while unintended consequences and adversary return-on-investment are minimized. These methods will support risk trade-offs in homogeneous enterprise systems in the near-term, and integrated heterogeneous cyber-physical systems in the mid-term. In the long term, they will enable integrated resilient architectures that are optimized for the ability to absorb shocks and speed recovery to a known secure operable state. Focus areas include:

- Autonomous reconfiguration and movement of resources to enable changing cyber assets to be marshaled and directed in order to create a defensive advantage.

- Transparent direct remediation and indirect mitigation of damage. Direct remediation mechanisms isolate damaged or compromised components and systems and provide (via alternate mechanisms, if necessary) essential functionality transparently to end users. Direct remediation will thwart irreparable harm to assets (e.g., destruction or indeterminate corruption) and degradation of critical operations. Indirect mitigation includes recovering, repairing, reconstituting, or replacing potentially compromised components, information flows, or systems, and applying supply chain analysis and reverse engineering so that components can be identified and at scale.

- Application of social science for security, including manipulation of adversary perceptions of cyber effects (e.g., via denial and deception techniques) in order to influence the adversary's knowledge of, and confidence in, the effectiveness of their cyber operations.

Coordination at multiple scales. Provide methods to manage risks at multiple scales (component, device, system, systems of systems, enterprise, or international coalition) and enable comprehensive and collective responses to specific types of malicious cyber activities, such as DDoS attacks. These methods support the collection of threat intelligence in the near-term, coordination of defensive activities in the mid-term, and negotiation and orchestration of collective defenses in the long-term. Focus areas include:

- Collection and production of fused, multi-source threat intelligence and information sharing that can provide cyber defenders with accurate risk assessments, accomplished by means such as privacy-preserving data analytics.

- Orchestrated autonomous or semi-autonomous defensive activities to counter system destabilization (e.g., cascading failures), especially of cyber-physical systems.

- Automated negotiation and orchestration of recovery and resilience courses of action to enable cyber defenders to avoid system destabilization or adversarial manipulation, including during large-scale adversary cyber operations (e.g., large-scale DDoS operations).

- Federated coordination of cyber defenses across organizational boundaries. This includes both technical and social science approaches, such as for decentralized command and control, "no fault" discussions for complex diagnostics, and lessons-learned activities.

<u>R&D Objectives</u>

Near-term:

- Develop the technologies and techniques that enable critical assets to adjust and continue operating acceptably, despite adversary actions.

Mid-term:

- Establish methods to achieve the timely recovery of functionality of inter-dependent systems even while adversary activity continues.

Long-term:

- Build adaptive effective collective defenses informed by predictive analysis that minimize adversary-imposed effects, as well as unintended effects caused by defender actions.

4. Emerging Technologies and Applications

The previous section defined four elements for effective cybersecurity. These elements are universally applicable and are needed to achieve cybersecurity in all technical contexts. The details for providing these elements may differ depending on the specific context.

This section reviews emerging technologies and identifies R&D priorities associated with that specific technical context. The examples have economic and national security implications, but the list is not exhaustive. Similar analysis can and should be performed for any technology—new, old, or emerging.

Cyber-Physical Systems and the Internet of Things

Cyber-Physical Systems (CPS) are smart, networked systems with embedded sensors, processors, and actuators that are designed to sense and interact with the physical world (including human users) and support real-time, guaranteed performance in safety-critical applications. CPS systems are an increasing part of all national critical infrastructures, finding new applications of CPS technology to improve everyday life and even transforming views of a society and community.

Very early examples of CPS are SCADA (supervisory control and data acquisition) systems that used dedicated communication channels to enable remote control of large industrial equipment. These early systems were very specialized proprietary systems, separated from the Internet and its risks, and used for remote control of, for example, electrical generators and power transmission and distribution. The economic advantages of the Internet and increasing functionality of commodity networking and information technology, however, incentivized re-architecting SCADA systems, unfortunately now raising cybersecurity concerns.

SCADA systems today are no longer walled-off from the threats of the Internet or vulnerabilities in networking and information technologies. Cybersecurity risks now affect the safety and availability of the services provided by critical infrastructures. The threats include purposefully coordinated existential threats to national critical infrastructures.

The emerging industry of IoT is equally affected. IoT refers to physical devices with electronics and software that can be sensed, controlled, and easily interoperated over the Internet. These devices have become the staple of home automation, especially Internet-controllable home lighting, heating, cooling, and security systems. The *2014 NSTAC Report to the President on the Internet of Things* projected a staggering 26-to-50 billion IoT devices will be deployed in manufacturing, business, and home applications by 2020.[36] Cybersecurity will be a daunting challenge at this unprecedented scale with low-end commodity networked devices in many diverse applications.

Cybersecurity risks to the safety of IoT and CPS systems, if unaddressed, will impede and block their adoption by society, preventing the full benefits of this technology from being realized for national priorities.

Cloud Computing

The last decade has seen an expansion of computing onto new kinds of platforms, bringing along with it an expansion of new cybersecurity threats. Commercial cloud computing is one such new platform. In cloud-computing platforms, a service provider maintains a large computing and storage infrastructure in one or more data centers and rents the use of this infrastructure to users, who access it over the Internet.

[36]http://www.dhs.gov/sites/default/files/publications/NSTAC%20Report%20to%20the%20President%20on%20the%20Internet%20of%20Things%20Nov%202014%20%28updat%20%20%20.pdf

Cloud-computing platforms have all the cybersecurity concerns of traditional systems where each user maintained their own entirely separate computing infrastructure, in addition to new concerns stemming from the sharing of computing infrastructure in the cloud.

Cloud-computing platforms typically use virtualization to execute computation owned by different users on the same shared hardware and software infrastructure. Virtualization is a technique that supports the illusion that each user has an exclusive use of the computer, when in reality one computer may be splitting its time serving several users. Adversaries can potentially exploit flaws in virtualization to pierce this illusion to access or infer other users' data. The potential to exploit these flaws, coupled with the high degree of network connectivity between computers in a data center, increases the threat that a single adversary armed with the knowledge of a relatively small set of exploitable flaws might harm many customers.

Cloud computing will benefit from broad advances in cybersecurity research in each of the four elements, but targeted research to assess, measure, and verify the protections provided by virtualization techniques will be required for a complete picture.

High Performance Computing

High performance computing (HPC) is essential to the Nation's economic competitiveness, scientific discovery, and national security. In July 2015, EO 13702 established the National Strategic Computing Initiative (NSCI), a whole-of-government effort to advance the full range of HPC technologies and extend HPC access to new business and scientific domains. The NSCI also envisions collaborative efforts with academia and the private sector to complement Federal investments, resulting in a whole-of-nation effort.

Advancing the efficacy and efficiency of HPC cybersecurity controls has been identified as a key technology goal for the NSCI. Like cyber-physical systems, access to supercomputers and networks has traditionally been tightly controlled through physical measures. HPC applications were often designed to operate in a serial fashion, requiring unfettered access to all the computing resources to maximize their computing power. Security controls consumed precious compute cycles without contributing directly towards the task at hand, so their application was relatively limited. HPC network access has become commonplace, as new applications emerge leveraging massive scientific data sets collected by sensors or scientific instruments, and new HPC systems support execution of applications in parallel. This new complexity has heightened HPC security requirements, while the existing pressure to maximize performance remains. New research is needed to determine whether traditional security mechanisms will be effective for the next generation of HPC systems called for by the NSCI, without incurring undue financial costs or performance degradation. If traditional mechanisms are ineffective or inefficient, new technologies will be needed to avoid the consequences of inadequate security (e.g., loss of confidentiality, integrity, or availability, or destruction of data).

Autonomous Systems

Technologies for autonomous systems and components are maturing and their security implications have been raised often. Research challenges for autonomous systems include manipulation of machine learning algorithms and resulting effects on resilience. In the near-term, semi-autonomous systems provide functionality; complete autonomy will largely be moderated by humans in the loop and the emphasis will be on IT management (e.g., performance optimization) and security (e.g., automated response). The mid-term will see semi-autonomous systems of systems that integrate cyber-physical systems and IT (e.g., self-driving vehicles), and autonomy will be moderated not by humans in the loop, but by the ability to orchestrate the system. The long-term will see largely autonomous systems of systems that integrate cyber-physical systems and IT at multiple scales and with varying degrees of autonomy, ranging from micro-robotic swarms to smart cities.

<u>Mobile Devices</u>

Traditionally, users and administrators accessed computers from terminals, system consoles, and desktop workstations. While laptops allowed some mobility, network access usually required a physical connection such as a telephone or Ethernet jack. These constraints have been shattered by the introduction of wireless networking and ubiquitous handheld devices (e.g., smart phones and tablets). BYOD and teleworking initiatives have accelerated these trends. Further, there are more stakeholders involved in achieving security today, including component and device manufacturers, operating system designers and developers, application developers, cloud storage providers, and network providers. While many of the broad advances in cybersecurity technologies will apply to these devices, mobility creates new challenges for protection (e.g., secure update), detection, and situational awareness.

5. Critical Dependencies

Advancements in areas on which cybersecurity critically depends are integral to the development of the four elements. The focus here is on the four elements, their relationship with each dependency, and advances that would contribute to attaining the goals of this Plan.

5.1 Scientific Foundations

Developing scientific foundations was a research theme in the 2011 Plan and still remains important for achieving this Plan's goals and objectives. In today's increasingly networked, distributed, and asynchronous world, cybersecurity involves hardware, software, networks, data, people, and integration with the physical world. Vulnerabilities in one part of a complex system are often used by malicious adversaries to exploit other parts in the system. Heuristic methods are inadequate for developing trusted systems that maintain desired functionality and can accommodate evolving technologies and threats. Such methods often are ad hoc, incomplete, and miss important vulnerabilities; the persistent adversary can often exploit the systems that use such assurance methods. Cybersecurity based on the four elements needs sound mathematical and scientific foundations with clear objectives, comprehensive theories (e.g., of defense, systems, and adversaries), principled design methodologies, models of complex and dynamic systems at multiple scales, and metrics for evaluating success or failure.

In the current state of the art, scientifically established and well-understood solutions exist unevenly in various security subdomains. Most techniques are domain- and context-specific, often not validated as mathematically and empirically sound, and rarely take into account efficacy and efficiency. Thus, the state of the practice consists of heuristic techniques, informal principles and models of presumed adversary behavior, and process-oriented metrics. Establishing scientific foundations in the areas below will directly support the goals and objectives for the four elements:

- Formal frameworks for the four elements with quantitative definitions of threats, measurable security assumptions and guarantees, and efficient formal methods for evaluating compositions of systems, defenses, and adversaries.

- Principled design techniques to construct security ecosystems for the four elements with provable or measurable verification and validation of security properties, and characterizations of efficiency.

- Reasoning frameworks to anticipate evolving and disruptive technologies and threats.

5.2 Risk Management

Technologies associated with the four elements *enable* cybersecurity, but *achieving* appropriate levels of security requires more than technology. The application of these technologies requires significant insight into an organization's goals, its abilities and modalities, and the nature of the threats it faces. Risk management is the ongoing process of identifying, assessing, and responding to risk. To manage risk, organizations should understand the likelihood that an event will occur and the resulting impact so they can determine an acceptable level of risk tolerance. This information is essential in making informed investments with scarce cybersecurity dollars.

Risk management is a relatively mature field, with widely accepted processes and a variety of risk models. National Institute of Standards and Technology (NIST) Special Publication 800-39 presents a generally accepted process, consistent with international standards, for information-security risk management at all levels of an organization.[37] The NIST Framework for Improving Critical Infrastructure Cybersecurity presents a flexible framework to help organizations manage and reduce cybersecurity risk, and has been applied across a broad spectrum of organizations in terms of size (including small and medium-sized businesses) and maturity (i.e., differing levels of cybersecurity). These methods can be applied (individually and in coordination) to a variety of trust and governance models.

While risk management practices offer significant value, the return on investment has historically been influenced by complex and decentralized risk governance, uncertainty in risk assessment techniques, and inaccurate cost estimation. The authority, responsibility, and decision-making power for information risk management are often distributed, resulting in a delayed, fragmentary, or uncoordinated response to risks. Uncertainty in risk assessment techniques is compounded by an inability in traditional models to accurately express that uncertainty. The lifecycle costs of security solutions are often underappreciated with respect to operations and management costs and especially for weak solutions.

Advances in risk management are needed to achieve the R&D objectives of the four elements. In particular, integrated cost modeling techniques are needed that incorporate human factors, such as required expertise and ongoing training, and risk models that incorporate information about the known and projected vulnerabilities. In the long term, it is necessary to better inform risk management by integrating modeling, simulation, and exercises into its practice.

5.3 Human Aspects

Experts estimate that 80-90 percent of current cybersecurity failures are due to human and organizational shortcomings.[38] Comprehensive cybersecurity requires understanding the human facets of cyber threats and secure cyber systems. Much research in social, behavioral, and economic disciplines has investigated the human aspects of cybersecurity problems. The field of cybersecurity economics examines adversaries' incentives and the means by which they profit from malicious cyber activities in the real world. The economic analysis of incentives helps explain why individuals and organizations do (and do not) take action to detect and mitigate cybersecurity threats. Social psychologists have investigated the impact of individual characteristics (e.g., age, gender, dispositional factors of personality) and social norms on promoting good practices in cyberspace. Research on persuasion has identified methods to train, incentivize, or encourage users to improve their cybersecurity behavior. Socio-technical investigations have expanded understanding of the role of trust and assurance in secure socio-technical systems as well as deception and adverse intentions in malicious cyber activities. While these are excellent examples of fruitful multi-disciplinary research activities, many opportunities in the economic, human, and social research still exist for improving cybersecurity. Research in the areas below is needed to support the four elements:

- Research in economic ecosystem externalities to enable understanding of the impact of trust and organizational design on cybersecurity decisions, as well as the role of micro- and macroeconomics in the design, construction, and operation of software, hardware, and systems.

- Modeling and social and behavioral experimentation to help identify the strengths and weaknesses of incentive mechanisms to acquire and deploy cybersecurity measures.

---

[37] http://csrc.nist.gov/publications/nistpubs/800-39/SP800-39-final.pdf

[38] For example, in a 2014 IBM report, over 95 percent of all (cybersecurity) incidents investigated recognize "human error" as a contributing factor. See http://media.scmagazine.com/documents/82/ibm_cyber_security_intelligenc_20450.pdf.

- Development of validated sociological models of human weaknesses and strengths for use in analyzing security properties in systems and the respective roles of users, developers, operators, defenders, and adversaries. There is also a need to identify and teach human behaviors that enhance security and identify effective methods to encourage more cyber-secure behavior in the design and operation of IT systems.

- Modeling international norms, rules of engagement, and escalation dynamics of malicious cyber activities to cyber-warfare to enable identification of institutional and structural factors that promote or undermine a secure cyberspace.

- Preventing and detecting insider threats by designing systems, both human and technical, that can better identify insiders doing harm to their organizations in real-time, rather than after the fact as is common today.

- Research in usable security in order to be able to design security techniques that optimize cognitive efficiency.

- Validated modeling and practices for team composition, coordination across teams, and integrated activities between diverse stakeholders in order to greatly increase the effectiveness of collective actions in the four elements.

- Development of validated models of varied adversary motives, responses, and susceptibility to deterrence actions such as denial, attribution, and retaliation. Understanding and anticipating adversary reaction to defensive actions and discovering their vulnerability to misinformation and confusion would further serve to reverse their asymmetric advantage.

5.4 Transition to Practice

Federal R&D spending in the cybersecurity arena remains a high national priority and ensuring the transition of research into practice is essential to maximizing return on investments. Accelerating transition to practice was a research theme in the 2011 plan and remains an important aspect of the current Plan.

As reported in the June 2014 "Report on Implementing the Federal Cybersecurity Research and Development Strategy," a gap exists between the research community, which focuses on the study and development of new cyber technologies and practices, and the operations community, which acquires system prototypes and implements them in operational environments.[39] Bridging that chasm requires synergistic efforts and investments by both the R&D and operations communities, and it may mean risk-taking for the private sector as it shepherds research results through the commercialization process. The Federal research community should continue activities outlined in the 2011 plan to expand transitions to practice via technology discovery, testing, evaluation and transition, commercialization, and workforce training.

Federal agencies should continue to allocate R&D funding to transition-to-practice activities, such as System Integrator Forums, Small Business Innovation Research (SBIR) activities, and consortium ventures.

Transition to practice is also a social and behavioral challenge. The 2015 Adoption of Cybersecurity Technologies Workshop report noted that "...early engagement among all stakeholders is critical, a

---

[39] https://www.nitrd.gov/PUBS/ImplFedCybersecurityRDStrategy-June2014.pdf

technology or best practice needs a champion, developers need to understand user needs and decision-maker concerns, [and] human factors, such as resistance to change, need to be considered by developers, decision-makers and implementers."[40] Further research in these aspects will facilitate the coordination among Chief Information Officers (CIOs), Chief Information Security Officers (CISOs), procurement officers, and Federal IT managers that will be needed to identify, develop, and deploy appropriate technologies.

Streamlining and accelerating the acquisition process for the results of R&D should also remain a priority. Agencies should continue to assess and selectively utilize all contractual instruments at their disposal. For example, Other Transactions (OTs) can provide a mechanism to streamline and accelerate funding of R&D and also allow agencies to reach performers who are typically not engaged in government-funded research. Reducing the time it takes to obtain patents and trademarks will also accelerate technology innovation and development.

Harmonizing technology transfer processes across Federal agencies would also improve the transition of research into practice. For example, there is no uniform approach for the private sector to license technology developed by the government. Streamlining these processes would significantly eliminate some of the obstacles and accelerate the transfer of technology.

5.5 Workforce Development

Developing and retaining the necessary cybersecurity workforce remains a key challenge. People are an essential component of cyber systems and can contribute to their security (or insecurity) in a variety of ways. The success or failure of this Plan depends largely upon three components of the national workforce: cybersecurity researchers, product developers, and cybersecurity professionals.

The growing demand for cybersecurity professionals is well documented, and appropriate efforts are already underway. The National Initiative for Cybersecurity Education (NICE)[41] was established in 2010 to implement recommendations of the Cyberspace Policy Review[42] and Comprehensive National Cybersecurity Initiative.[43] It is leading a robust portfolio of Federal efforts to satisfy the cybersecurity workforce needs of government and the private sector. NICE coordinates government workforce programs in cybersecurity education, training, and workforce development across more than 20 different Federal departments and agencies; collaborates with industry to understand its cybersecurity workforce needs; and engages with K-12 schools and academia to establish innovative curriculum, degree programs, and experiential learning.

To satisfy national needs for a robust and productive workforce, however, the cybersecurity profession must attract and retain talent from previously untapped applicant pools, change the image of the field by celebrating innovations in cybersecurity, and increase the appeal of the field to a diverse audience of workers. Innovative solutions to national cybersecurity R&D challenges will come from a diversity of perspectives and by fostering the American entrepreneurial spirit.

---

[40] http://cps-vo.org/node/19093

[41] http://csrc.nist.gov/nice/index.htm

[42] https://www.whitehouse.gov/assets/documents/Cyberspace_Policy_Review_final.pdf

[43] https://www.whitehouse.gov/issues/foreign-policy/cybersecurity/national-initiative

A critical cornerstone of secure cyber systems is the recognition that cybersecurity is a shared responsibility borne by researchers, developers, administrators, and users. The common image of the cybersecurity professional as a warfighter, computer "geek," or secret operative, however, appeals to only a minority of potential workers that possess or would consider developing cyber skills. Significant pools of talent have opted out of the cybersecurity workforce, creating a lack of candidates for competitive positions and, equally important, potentially hindering innovation through a lack of diversity of perspectives, problem solving skills, and experience.[44] Expanding the applicant pool by engaging women, under-represented ethnic and racial groups, and people with disabilities is essential to meeting the emerging workforce skills gaps. The Nation must promote training, education, and career development opportunities in cybersecurity fields among the current, entering, and re-entering workforce across all sectors to satisfy present and future workforce demand and supply of qualified cybersecurity workers.

One of the recurring themes in this Plan is measuring the efficacy and efficiency of cybersecurity tools and techniques. Developing the capacity for this type of research within the cybersecurity research community is essential to the success of this R&D Plan. Cybersecurity researchers should acquire skills to adopt efficacy and efficiency as essential components for all cybersecurity research and curriculum development.

This Plan emphasizes the importance of reducing vulnerabilities in IT across the board. Vulnerabilities can only be reduced if developers accept cybersecurity as an essential requirement, adopt assurance-based design and development techniques and tool chains, and incorporate sound security update mechanisms. Developing a software development workforce that recognizes the importance of low-vulnerability IT systems and products and has the skills to achieve that goal, is essential to the success of this Plan.

The community of developers and product architects that needs to understand cybersecurity will continue to grow. For example, medical device designers will need to recognize the interconnected nature of their devices and incorporate cybersecurity protections as well. As the range and scope of cyberspace continues to expand, new workforces must be prepared to integrate cybersecurity technologies and concepts into their fields.

5.6 Research Infrastructure

Access to advanced cybersecurity testbeds continues to be a hurdle for researchers. Testbeds are essential so that researchers can use actual operational data to model and conduct experiments on real-world system vulnerabilities and exploitation scenarios in proper test environments. These models and experimental methods must be shared and validated by the research community by giving them access to these test environments. Current experimental analysis tools, however, are often custom built on an ad-hoc basis, experiment by experiment. Stand-alone testbeds in niche areas of cybersecurity abound but do not enable comprehensive experimentation with inputs from a diversity of human and technological sources. Cybersecurity experimentation must include the ability to capture, model, and

---

[44] According to the 2013 report, Agents of Change: Women in the Information Security Profession, women represent just 11% of the cybersecurity workforce. The RSA Conference panel presentation "Building the Bridge Across the Great Minority Cyber Divide" reported that the combined percentage of Hispanics and African Americans in cybersecurity is less than 10% of the workforce. See https://www.isc2cares.org/uploadedFiles/wwwisc2caresorg/Content/Women-in-the-Information-Security-Profession-GISWS-Subreport.pdf and https://www.rsaconference.com/writable/presentations/file_upload/prof-m04_building-the-bridge-across-the-great-minority-cyber-divide.pdf

recreate realistic human behaviors. Current methods fall short of realistically integrating human factors into experiments and accurately quantifying them as a security variable to be tested.

Data repositories exist today, but many are unable to deal with proliferation of massive data sets, do not support semantically rich data searches and have limited data provenance information. Furthermore, static repositories are of limited value for resilience research, where dynamic, agile repositories are needed. Understanding data provenance is crucial for research and enabling others to reproduce research results on other datasets. In addition, researchers lack access to realistic social media and insider threat data to conduct human behavior analyses, in order to refine technical solutions and policies in these areas.

Due to the vast disparities in system requirements, no single testbed can suffice for all types of cybersecurity research. Stand-alone, sector-specific testbeds offer limited support for research experimentation on inter-dependencies. Such testbeds are proprietary and closed to all but a handful of researchers, and are often not Internet-accessible. A broad array of versatile, non-sector-specific testbeds are needed to enable better testing of methods and procedures as well as standards for testbed interconnection to support complex, large scale activities.

Further, research in cybersecurity requires realistic experimental data which emulates insider threat, external adversary activities, and defensive behavior, in terms of both technological systems and human decision making. The integrity and availability of such data sets is crucial to ensuring scientifically reliable results. Data collection, however, must observe all appropriate laws and regulations and should be ethically conducted.[45] There is a substantial lack of vetted, provenance-detailed, and openly available data sets that are needed in order to obtain research reproducibility, an inherent trait of the science of security. Special, one-off relationships with industry partners to acquire access to their proprietary data means that a broader pool of researchers cannot utilize the data or peer review the results.

Cyber-threat data sharing for operational purposes is crucial in the defense against malicious cyber activities. Such data sharing also has vital strategic benefits to enable research of new, effective ways to protect critical information systems. Currently, data owners possessing real, high-fidelity data are reluctant to share such data for government-funded research. Data owners take on risk when sharing their data with researchers—disclosures of events could damage their reputation and impact business or the public. There is also no accepted safe method for data de-identification to implement privacy and confidentiality protections specifically for research. Aggressive de-identification can make data less useful to researchers, while too little precaution could result in an inadvertent disclosure of personal information, proprietary information, or other sensitive data. There is a need for a plan that supports responsible high-fidelity data sharing for innovative cybersecurity research, providing protections (e.g., indemnification, transfer of liability) to those organizations that voluntarily share this data with researchers after applying accepted de-identification methods. Encouraging cyber-related data sharing for government-funded cybersecurity research through appropriate safeguards for subjects of data and protections for data owners would likely stimulate innovative approaches and solutions.

The Federal Government, with industry participation, should expand the scope and fidelity of cybersecurity testbeds in cloud computing, manufacturing, electrical power, transportation, information and networking systems, healthcare, and telecommunications. It should also enable multi-disciplinary experimentation in computer science, engineering, mathematics, modeling, human behavior, sociology, economics, epistemology, and education.

---

[45] *The Menlo Report: Ethical Principles Guiding Information and Communication Technology Research*, August 2012, http://www.dhs.gov/sites/default/files/publications/CSD-MenloPrinciplesCORE-20120803_1.pdf

6. Implementing the Plan

This section reviews the roles and responsibilities of Federal agencies, the private sector, universities and other research organizations for implementing the Plan in 2016 and beyond. It describes existing coordination and planning mechanisms within the private and public sectors and outlines priorities for and possible obstacles to advancing cybersecurity R&D.

6.1   Roles and Responsibilities

Research and development funding is a scarce resource, regardless of source. For this reason, it is essential to invest wisely and selectively to avoid research redundancies. This section identifies the respective roles for the Federal Government, private industry, academia, and research organizations and identifies strategies and vehicles for ensuring coordination among sectors. All organizations must comply with applicable laws and ethics of research. Chief Privacy Officers have unique opportunities to help researchers and program managers conduct productive research that protects and enhances civil liberties.

Federal Research Agencies

The Federal Government has a dual role with regards to its support for R&D. It is the primary source of funding for long-term, high-risk research initiatives but also funds near-term developmental work to meet department- or agency-specific requirements or important public goods that industry is not incented to pursue. Achieving and maintaining the appropriate balance between the two is an ongoing process and the appropriate balance point differs for different agencies.

Science agencies, such as the National Science Foundation (NSF) and National Institute of Standards and Technology (NIST), have a leading role in funding cybersecurity R&D to support this Plan. In keeping with their science missions, these agencies focus on basic and longer-term, higher-risk research. Depending upon the agency, the research may be executed in-house, at national laboratories, or in academia via grants, other transactions, cooperative agreements, or contracts. The challenge for these agencies is twofold: identifying and funding the most promising and important R&D initiatives and transitioning this research into practice. Science agencies will utilize this Plan as the foundation for funding decisions but should also adjust their decision-making as cyber policies and threats evolve. Science agencies should embrace and fund multi-disciplinary research, and continue to demand strong scientific methods in all funded initiatives. They should support foundational research, yet also research that produces data that support the efficacy and efficiency of new techniques or practices so as to contribute to the Plan's vision.

Mission agencies primarily fund applied research with a near-term or mid-term horizon to meet immediate and future mission requirements. Mission-specific R&D is often incremental in nature, and agencies should make special efforts to ensure that the desired functionality is not already available from the private sector (nor from other Federal agencies). Research arms of these mission agencies may also support basic and long term research activities with potential to significantly impact agency missions within their portfolio.

Both science and mission agencies should avoid funding near-term R&D unless it is directly related to mission-specific needs or creates public goods that industry is not incented to pursue. Near-term, broadly applicable R&D is best done within private industry, as it is better positioned to shape and respond to market demands.

Government scientists, national laboratories, and Federally Funded Research and Development Centers (FFRDCs) are positioned to perform long-term high-risk research. These organizations exist to perform research that is too sensitive or too risky for the private sector, and are capable of doing this across multiple disciplines.

With these research performers, however, there are only limited paths for transition to commercial practice. Technologies may become products custom-tailored for the government and satisfy specific mission requirements. In order to have impacts outside the government, Federal agencies should make partnerships with industry.

Private Sector

The budgets for commercially-funded cybersecurity research are usually comparatively modest for even the largest IT companies. Private-sector R&D funding typically is internal and focused on product-development goals based on the specific needs of the company as well as on profitability and turnaround time. While companies often have the skills to perform longer-term higher-risk research, the opportunity cost of moving personnel to address these topics is high, even when government funding is available to defray the immediate costs, because longer-term research often benefits the entire industry and not just the company that funded it. Nonetheless, there are opportunities for the R&D activities of the private and public sectors to be synergistic and complementary. A well-functioning cybersecurity research ecosystem must offer several mechanisms for the two to mutually benefit from each other.

Most companies that have laboratories or groups that are actively pursuing R&D and applications of cybersecurity technologies, tools, and methods are from the IT and telecommunications sectors. Cybersecurity, however, is not just a problem of IT and telecommunications: important cybersecurity R&D is underway at companies producing medical equipment, automotive systems, and avionics. Yet other sectors, such as banking, manufacturing, power, and agriculture can bring value to the research space by working with researchers on long-term issues, providing access to real-world data, and supporting research through funding.

Cybersecurity is not only a problem for big companies, but also for small and medium businesses (SMB). While it is unreasonable to expect SMB to have their own research programs, participating in academic or private-sector programs will help focus researchers on the needs of organizations with limited IT capacity.

Opportunity for fruitful collaboration exists in expanding efforts to measure and verify efficacy and efficiency in cybersecurity products and services. Consumers and enterprises need such information for effective and efficient management of their cybersecurity risks. Indeed, there is a growing awareness in the private sector that compliance-based approaches are not working: cybersecurity needs to be integrated into the broader IT environment and focused on addressing the more important business risks.[46] Private-sector product vendors should consider the full range of costs of using cybersecurity solutions, from financial costs to cognitive load on users to innovation-inhibiting practices. Another fruitful partnership opportunity would be to jointly identify pre-competitive research areas in which private-public partnership funding would be most productive.

Academia and Research Organizations

Academia is the leading R&D performer of basic research and longer-term, higher-risk initiatives. It is the source for new ideas in cybersecurity. Academics are strongly encouraged to embrace this Plan's focus

---

[46] World Economic Forum and McKinsey & Co., "Risk and Responsibility in a Hyperconnected World", January 2014.

on measurable and testable efficacy and efficiency. Where possible, efficacy metrics against open data sets (such as PREDICT[47]) should be provided to enable comparison and evaluation of competing techniques. Use of open data sets also enables reproducibility of experiments, which is a basic tenet in other scientific disciplines. Academic researchers are also encouraged to incorporate strategies for transitioning successful research into practice when developing proposals and initiating research.

Academia also strongly influences research directions through the promotion and tenure process. Academic institutions are strongly encouraged to value multi-disciplinary cybersecurity research, even where publication occurs in non-traditional journals for the field. Institutions are also encouraged to value research with rigorously-defined models and experimental design.

Research organizations and professional societies are a natural partner in these efforts. They produce research strategies, organize conferences, and publish journals. By establishing publication requirements for documented efficacy and efficiency, these organizations can greatly aid and improve scientific rigor in the cybersecurity field (e.g., by publishing detailed results on experiment methods, measurement techniques, and failed research).

International Partners

Existing efforts in science diplomacy and collaborations with international partners provide an opportunity to complement Federal and private-sector R&D efforts in cybersecurity. Cybersecurity is a global concern, and the United States should leverage other countries' cybersecurity R&D investments and vice versa. This Plan should guide discussions in international technical and inter-governmental meetings so that international cybersecurity R&D investments can complement Federal R&D investments.

Coordination and Collaboration

Coordination and collaboration across sectors is essential to avoiding redundant research initiatives. This coordination should occur at several levels: among departments and agencies; among government, private industry, and academia; and among international partners.

The Federal cybersecurity R&D community does engage with industry via many different mechanisms in the form of public-private partnerships. For example, the Trusted Computing Group is a partnership that provides technology for hardware-based cryptography, key repositories, self-encrypting drives, and device authentication. NSF co-funds research with the Semiconductor Research Corporation (SRC) to support the development of secure, trustworthy and resilient semiconductors. Research alliances can draw together industry leaders to address shared cybersecurity problems and to foster strategies for transformative solutions to these problems. Agencies have also used advisory boards to obtain an industry perspective, such as the NIST Information Security and Privacy Advisory Board. The Department of Homeland Security (DHS) has hosted a dozen National Conversations on a Trusted Cyber Future throughout the country to engage industry leaders. Both DHS and the Department of Defense (DoD) have opened offices in Silicon Valley to expand their conversations with technology innovators. The Federal R&D community also has relationships with the private sector in areas such as cognitive systems, big data, social networking, privacy, cryptography, predictive analytics, search, cloud computing, and software. In addition, there is also National Cybersecurity Center of Excellence (NCCoE) FFRDC, sponsored by NIST to accelerate the adoption of secure technologies.

---

[47] The Protected Repository for the Defense of Infrastructure Against Cyber Threats. See https://www.predict.org/

Coordination between departments and agencies is facilitated by the NSTC. Unclassified Federal research and development efforts in networking and information technology are coordinated by the NITRD Program, supported by the National Coordination Office (NCO) for NITRD. Classified research efforts are coordinated by the NSTC's Special Cyber Operations and Research Engineering (SCORE) subcommittee.

6.2   Implementation Roadmap

The coordinated R&D activities of this plan are carried out by a number of Federal agencies with varying missions but complementary roles. Among the agencies, for example, NSF supports academic research, DARPA focuses on high-risk efforts that both prevent and create technical surprise, DoD Service research organizations focus on their respective mission requirements, and DHS supports applied research in the context of homeland security and securing the Nation's critical infrastructures. This arrangement assures that the full spectrum of R&D approaches is represented and engaged.

Accordingly, each agency structures its R&D activities based on its mission and resources. Each agency should, in collaboration with the Office of Management and Budget (OMB), with other White House organizations as needed, and with Congress, incorporate the objectives of this Plan into its research plans and programs as appropriate. Details of R&D carried out by each agency involved are provided by agencies through their appropriate venues, such as agency-specific strategic plans or implementation roadmaps and via appropriate contracting methods such as solicitations or broad agency announcements (BAAs).

The agencies should engage industry and academics through their individual programs, such as BAAs from DARPA and DHS, public working groups from NIST, and program solicitations from NSF. Each year, the NITRD Program compiles and produces a Supplement to the President's Budget (published at https://www.nitrd.gov), which provides highlights of agency activities and research activities in various areas of IT and networking. In the supplement, the Cyber Security and Information Assurance (CSIA) section provides an overview of the ongoing unclassified Federal investment in cybersecurity R&D. The CSIA section provides information about the activities and investments the agencies are pursuing in implementing this Plan. In addition, the agencies should work through NITRD to coordinate their activities under the Plan and reach out to industry and academia to promulgate the Plan via academic workshops and inviting academics and industry representatives to talk with agency representatives.

7. Recommendations

The Federal Government in its entirety can support this Plan and achieve its vision by supporting the following recommendations:

Recommendation 1: Prioritize basic and long-term research in Federal cybersecurity R&D.

Given the increasing value to the Nation created and enabled by the Internet, there should be a higher priority assigned to R&D to protect that value. Current investments in cybersecurity R&D are not keeping pace with the increase in risk, and have not satisfied society's needs for cybersecurity technologies that are effective and efficient.

The cybersecurity R&D community is active and growing. There are numerous annual world-class research conferences where results can be shared among the community. There is a solid base of R&D funding, including substantial Federal R&D funding as well as ongoing commercial R&D investments. The Nation as a whole would benefit from a steady increase in Federal and private-sector cybersecurity R&D, with a particular emphasis on basic research and long-term, high-risk research initiatives. Because basic research and long-term research especially are areas where the private sector is not likely to invest, Federal investments will be important for R&D in these areas.

Within Federal investments in IT R&D in general and cybersecurity R&D in particular, basic and long-term cybersecurity research should be prioritized. As basic research results mature and as long-term research initiatives become applicable to practice, then support for applied and near-term research, relying heavily on private resources, will also be appropriate.

Recommendation 2: Lower barriers and strengthen incentives for public and private organizations that would broaden participation in cybersecurity R&D.

Additional benefits come by augmenting Federal investments with increased private-sector investments in cybersecurity R&D. Continued data collection and study of the benefits expected and realized by the private sector from investment in cybersecurity would help motivate such investments and could identify classes of incentives that might be effective. A better understanding of the ways to incentivize industry to become more secure is as important to the adoption of cybersecurity techniques and measures as the effectiveness of the technologies themselves.

Federal agencies can lower the barriers to entry into the cybersecurity R&D marketplace by funding common research infrastructure (e.g. testbeds and data sets) in order to lower the cost of entry for small businesses, startup companies, and academic institutions and increase their participation in R&D. These organizations may have game-changing cyber security ideas but lack the financial assets to fund realistic design, modeling, and experimentation using relevant data.

Policymakers should review proposed laws, treaties, and regulations to understand how they impact ethical[48] cybersecurity R&D and consider engaging with relevant stakeholders to modify existing laws and regulations that may inhibit it.[49]

---

[48] *The Menlo Report: Ethical Principles Guiding Information and Communication Technology Research*, August 2012, http://www.dhs.gov/sites/default/files/publications/CSD-MenloPrinciplesCORE-20120803_1.pdf

[49] *Cybersecurity Research: Addressing the Legal Barriers and Disincentives.* From NSF-funded workshop, see, http://www.ischool.berkeley.edu/research/publications/2015/cybersecurity_research_addressing_legal_barriers_and_disincentives

Recommendation 3: Assess barriers and identify incentives that could accelerate the transition of evidence-validated effective and efficient cybersecurity research results into adopted technologies, especially for emerging technologies and threats.

Streamlining the technology transition process for Federally-funded research would encourage more private-sector companies to participate in R&D and transition their technologies. Federal agencies should work towards creating a suite of standardized licensing or other intellectual property agreements that could be selected to facilitate technology transfer for Federally-funded projects.

Utilizing the full range of tools that are in place to create more flexible and attractive technology transfer terms would encourage and enable the public to access and business to leverage government-funded research, including for commercialization.

Recommendation 4: Expand the diversity of expertise in the cybersecurity research community.

Cybersecurity needs extend beyond technology, requiring deep understanding of the human facets of cyber threats and secure cyber systems. To accelerate progress, the skills of traditional cybersecurity researchers should be augmented with expertise from social, behavioral, and economic disciplines.

Multi-disciplinary research should be promoted by funding agencies and by research institutions. Agencies should ensure that grant solicitations and grant review processes are open to multi-disciplinary proposals. Research institutions should ensure that advancement (e.g., tenure) decisions value multi-disciplinary research successes and publication in nontraditional journals and conferences equally with traditional tenure criteria.

Recommendation 5: Expand diversity in the cybersecurity workforce.

Diversity encompasses race, gender, ethnic group, age, personality, cognitive style, education, background, and more. Reframing the image of a cyber professional to be a more inclusive one would increase the talent pool, foster critical cyber skills among a wider swath of individuals, and promote a healthier, more culturally-sensitive workplace. A more diverse workforce can provide a richer set of perspectives and innovative solutions to problems. Research is needed to find ways to make cybersecurity a more attractive career option for many people and introduce greater diversity into recruiting and retention practices. Community-focused education campaigns should inform the public about the importance of cybersecurity and promote greater awareness and motivate young people to seek cybersecurity careers. Current professionals in the field should be encouraged to mentor and demonstrate the positive impacts their careers have in the social, economic, and national security sectors as well as the communities in which they work and live.

Harnessing the talent of an inclusive workforce with people of all backgrounds who are diverse in thought, experience, and skills is essential to enabling innovation and creative discovery. Organizational leaders should take measures to foster an inclusive workplace climate in cybersecurity to attract and recruit new talent, maximize employee engagement, and improve employee retention.

The Federal agencies should work with cybersecurity stakeholders to promote the visibility of cybersecurity careers and increase mobility of cybersecurity professionals across government, industry, and academia.

Acknowledgements

The Cybersecurity Research and Development Strategic Plan Working Group is grateful for everyone who provided input to this Plan. We recognize three contractors who each wrote important subsections, edited subsections, and provided extensive comments on the whole Plan: Nancy Forbes (for NITRD), Brendon Gibson (for DHS), and Vipin Swarup (for DoD). We also acknowledge the timely and thoughtful feedback we received from these reviewers: Marjory Blumenthal, Deb Bodeau, Megan Brewster, Rob Cunningham, Steve Fetter, Gabbi Fisher, Ben Flatgard, Erwin Gianchandani, Heather King, Jim Kirby, Paul Lopata, Marianne Swanson, Paul Timmel, Ralph Wachter, Cynthia Wright, and Heng Xu.

Abbreviations

BAA	Broad Area Announcement
CISR	Critical Infrastructure Security and Resilience
CPS	Cyber-Physical System
CSIA	Cyber Security and Information Assurance
DDoS	Distributed Denial of Service
DHS	Department of Homeland Security
DoD	Department of Defense
FFRDC	Federally Funded Research and Development Center
HPC	High Performance Computing
ICT	Information and Communications Technology
IoT	Internet of Things
IT	Information Technology
NICE	National Initiative for Cybersecurity Education
NIST	National Institute of Standards and Technology
NITRD	Networking and Information Technology Research and Development
NCO	National Coordination Office
NSF	National Science Foundation
NSTAC	National Security Telecommunications Advisory Committee
NSTC	National Science and Technology Council
NSTIC	National Strategy for Trusted Identities in Cyberspace
OT	Other Transactions
OSTP	Office of Science and Technology Policy
PPD	Presidential Policy Directive
PREDICT	Protected Repository for the Defense of Infrastructure Against Cyber Threats
R&D	Research and Development
SRC	Semiconductor Research Corporation
STEM	Science, Technology, Engineering, and Mathematics
S&T	Science and Technology
VPN	Virtual Private Network

Appendix A—Cybersecurity Enhancement Act Technical Objectives

The *Cybersecurity Enhancement Act of 2014* was a major impetus for the development of the Plan. In addition to directing development of Plan and setting a deadline for its publication, the Act included a list of technically-oriented cybersecurity objectives for consideration in the Plan. The list of objectives is reproduced below with a mapping of each objective to parts of the Plan.

Objectives

(A) How to design and build complex software-intensive systems that are secure and reliable when first deployed;

Ensuring that software and hardware are designed and implemented to minimize the number of vulnerabilities is a core tenet of the Protect element as defined in the Plan. A key long-term R&D objective for this element is the creation of development tool chains that efficiently produce software with only 1 percent of the vulnerabilities appearing in current COTS products:

> Obtain tool chains that support development of software with one defect per hundred thousand lines of code with a relative efficiency metric of 90% for productivity and system performance (i.e., systems with 1% of the defects in current systems that take no more than 10% longer to implement and run up to 10% slower).

(B) How to test and verify that software and hardware, whether developed locally or obtained from a third party, is free of significant known security flaws;

Two aspects of this objective are incorporated into the Protect element in the Plan. To enhance the security of existing code bases, the Plan prioritizes the development of efficient and effective static and dynamic software analysis tools. Researchers and consumers alike can apply these tools to open source code bases, and they are an important component of the software developer tool chains. To ensure that the products deployed are in fact the genuine article, the Plan also highlights the importance of objective measures for supply chain security.

In addition to the discussion in the text, the Plan establishes a mid-term R&D Objective to create static and dynamic analysis tools that reduce the number of vulnerabilities to 10 percent of the vulnerabilities appearing in current COTS products:

> Create tools for static and dynamic analysis that reduce vulnerabilities in traditionally developed code bases to one defect per ten thousand lines of code (i.e., develop testing tools that are sufficiently powerful to reduce the number of vulnerabilities in new and legacy code bases by a factor of ten).

(C) How to test and verify that software and hardware obtained from a third party correctly implements stated functionality, and only that functionality;

The Plan addresses this objective within the Protect element, under verify security and verify authenticity.

(D) How to guarantee the privacy of an individual, including that individual's identity, information, and lawful transactions when stored in distributed systems or transmitted over networks;

The Plan addresses this objective within the Protect element's security controls theme. Cryptography provides effective and efficient methods for safeguarding privacy and protecting confidentiality in a broad range of current systems and environments. In addition to existing mechanisms, this Plan highlights the importance of lightweight cryptography to support IoT and other resource constrained environments, the

Plan also highlights the importance of developing efficient privacy-preserving cryptographic mechanisms for particularly sensitive applications. The Plan identifies these advances as a near-term objective:

> Make cryptographic tools and techniques available for constrained environments (e.g., lightweight cryptography), privacy-sensitive applications (e.g., private databases), and lifetime confidentiality (e.g., quantum-resistant cryptography)

(E) How to build new protocols to enable the Internet to have robust security as one of the key capabilities of the Internet;

Ensuring that systems and protocols are designed to minimize the number of inherent weaknesses is a core tenet of the Protect element as defined in the Plan, and includes technologies such as correct computation and designing for correct operation of partially compromised systems.

(F) How to determine the origin of a message transmitted over the Internet;

Cryptographic authentication is the fundamental technology for verifying the source of a message. The Protect element includes both authentication and cryptographic security controls. The Detect element can facilitate determining origin and is most effective when considered in advance of designing systems.

(G) How to support privacy in conjunction with improved security;

This Plan is focused on development of elements for cybersecurity as traditionally defined: confidentiality, integrity, and availability. Achieving privacy R&D goals will be directly addressed in a forthcoming privacy and confidentiality strategy under development within NITRD.

While privacy R&D falls outside the core of this Plan, the Plan recognizes cybersecurity controls as essential to identify and mitigate privacy risks throughout the development life cycle of these controls. The Plan also postulates that security and privacy are not inherently in at odds with each, but recognizes that some security controls have implications for privacy. The Plan encourages developers of new cybersecurity controls to evaluate and document any implications for privacy and confidentiality.

(H) How to address the problem of insider threats;

This Plan does not explicitly differentiate between threats from insiders and external entities, jointly referring to them as "adversaries". While the insider's authorized access would simplify some activities, once the external adversary initially gains access they assume the authorizations of some user or process, essentially achieving the insider's initial state. The advanced security controls and reduction in vulnerabilities envisioned by the Protect element would limit lateral movement by all adversaries. The Detect element is more transformative; it identifies anomalous user behaviors or operates without relying on predefined attack signatures. Since insider malicious cyber activities may be constructed solely from authorized actions, this enhancement would significantly improve detection of insider threats.

(I) How improved consumer education and digital literacy initiatives can address human factors that contribute to cybersecurity;

Three parts of the workforce are identified as a dependency for this Plan: cybersecurity professionals; software and hardware developers; and cyber-physical product developers. The National Initiative for Cybersecurity Education (NICE) is the national program office for cybersecurity education, and for satisfying the cybersecurity workforce needs of the government and industry. The Plan also highlights the importance of education and literacy for software and hardware developers with respect to potential supply chain vulnerabilities. The Plan challenge academia to ensure that the next generation of product developers is fully versed in cybersecurity technologies. The Plan also notes the importance of cybersecurity education for product developers in manufacturing, power generation, and other critical infrastructure where IT is now integrated into components.

Cyber education and literacy are not the only means for addressing the human aspects of cybersecurity. The user assumption in Section 2 states that users will minimize efforts that do not directly contribute to the task at hand. Cyber-literate users may still reject cybersecurity tools (such as multi-factor authentication) due to the level of effort imposed by their use. In order to increase their acceptance and adoption, The Plan recommends research in social, behavioral, and economic sciences to enhance and document the efficiency of cybersecurity tools, especially their ease of use.

(J) How to protect information processed, transmitted, or stored using cloud computing or transmitted through wireless services;

Protection of information in cloud computing, wireless services, or other networked applications is addressed within the Protect element by the inclusion of cryptography within security controls. Cloud computing is also highlighted in the Section 4, Emerging Technologies and Applications.

(K) Include additional objectives the heads of the applicable agencies and departments, in coordination with the head of any relevant Federal agency and with input from stakeholders, including appropriate national laboratories, industry, and academia, determine appropriate.

This Plan incorporates additional objectives under the Deter and Adapt elements. The Deter element supports Federal, state, local, and tribal government roles (e.g. law enforcement) and recommends that system and network owners establish the efficacy of their overall defensive measures. The Adapt element incorporates two additional components of the NIST Cybersecurity Framework for Critical Infrastructure: Respond and Recover.

Appendix B—NIST Cybersecurity Framework Core

In 2014, NIST published the Framework for Improving Critical Infrastructure Cybersecurity. The NIST Cybersecurity Framework Core defines five functions (Identify, Protect, Detect, Respond, Recover), while this Plan defines four elements (Deter, Protect, Detect, and Adapt). The differences between the NIST functions and this Plan's elements are a consequence of the different scope and objectives associated with these documents, and do not introduce any incompatibility between these efforts. This Appendix provides a map between common parts and identifies differences due to scoping.

The Identify function and Deter element do not have exact complements in the two documents.

The Identify function in the NIST Framework establishes organizational understanding to support management of cybersecurity risks. The activities in the Identify function are foundational for achieving cybersecurity in practice, and must be factored into the design processes described within the Protect element. However, these techniques are more closely related to Risk Management, as described in the Critical Dependencies section of the Plan.

The Deter element describes technologies required to support deterrence through imposed costs on the adversary, such as legal prosecution and economic sanctions. Deterrence through imposed costs is the domain of Federal, state, and local authorities, and falls outside the scope of improving critical infrastructure cybersecurity. The remainder of the Deter element envisions technologies that measure an adversary's level of effort to ensure that costs outweigh the value of gains. While these technologies could be considered when implementing the Framework's Protect function, they do not provide protection by themselves.

The Framework's Protect and Detect functions map directly to the defensive elements with the same names in this Plan. The technologies this Plan seeks to develop would contribute directly to establishing or enhancing these functions.

The Framework's Respond and Recover functions map into a single element in this Plan: Adapt. The Respond function supports the ability to contain a cybersecurity incident, while Recover supports the ability to restore operations after the event. The Adapt element in this Plan envisions automated tools that contain incidents, continue or restore operations during incidents, and adjust the environment to preserve security and operational continuity in the face of ongoing or anticipated malicious cyber activities. Such automated tools demand integration of the respond, recover, and adjust components, so separate elements were not appropriate.

Appendix C—PPD-8: National Preparedness

As described below, this policy complements PPD-8 on National Preparedness of March 30, 2011.

Cyber preparedness is an essential part of the National Preparedness System across the prevention, protection, mitigation, response, and recovery mission areas established by PPD-8. By integrating cyber and traditional preparedness efforts, the Nation will be ready to manage incidents that include both cyber and physical effects. The advances in science and engineering envisioned by this Plan will contribute to national preparedness and support the National Incident Management System, when activated.

To clarify the contributions of the four elements described in this Plan, a mapping to the five mission areas in PPD-8 is provided below.

In PPD-8, prevention "refers to those capabilities necessary to avoid, prevent, or stop a threatened or actual" attack. Prevention operations are a subset of those operations that fall within the threat response category of efforts as defined in Section 2.D of this policy and are principally a government responsibility. The attribution technologies within this Plan's Deter element are a key enabler for threat response in the cyber or non-cyber domains. The Detect element contributes to PPD-8 prevention capabilities

In PPD-8, protection "refers to those capabilities necessary to secure the homeland against...manmade or natural disasters." Both physical and cyber protection activities are needed to secure key IT facilities and services from malicious cyber activity. The technology objectives detailed in this Plan's Protect element contribute directly to this goal.

In PPD-8, mitigation "refers to those capabilities necessary to reduce loss of life and property by lessening the impact of disasters [and includes]...efforts to improve the resilience of critical infrastructure [and]...risk reduction for specific vulnerabilities...." While this term is sometimes used in context of immediate network defense, under PPD-8, mitigation refers only to sustained risk management efforts intended to reduce the probability or lessen the impact of an incident. Risk management is highlighted as one of the Plan's critical dependencies, but is not one fop the four elements.

In PPD-8, response "refers to those capabilities necessary to save lives, protect property and the environment, and meet basic human needs after an incident has occurred." Response activities include the execution of emergency plans and actions to support short-term recovery. In this Plan, response is one of the integrated components of the Adapt element.

In PPD-8, recovery "refers to those capabilities necessary to...rebuilding infrastructure systems [and] ...restoring health, social, and community services...." In the cyber context, recovery is a follow-on activity to response, leading to the full restoration of the affected services and capacities. In this Plan, recovery is one of the integrated components of the Adapt element.